The Elements
of Expression

The
Elements of
Expression

PUTTING THOUGHTS
INTO WORDS

Arthur Plotnik

AN OWL BOOK
HENRY HOLT AND COMPANY
NEW YORK

Henry Holt and Company, Inc.
Publishers since 1866
115 West 18th Street
New York, New York 10011

Henry Holt® is a registered trademark
of Henry Holt and Company, Inc.

Published in Canada by Fitzhenry & Whiteside Ltd.,
195 Allstate Parkway, Markham, Ontario L3R 4T8.

Library of Congress Cataloging-in-Publication Data
Plotnik, Arthur.
        p.   cm.
Includes index and bibliographical references.
1. Oral communication.   2. Rhetoric.   I. Title.
            P95.P6   1996
302.2'242—dc20   95-42933
                                          CIP
            ISBN 0-8050-3774-8

Henry Holt books are available for special promotions and
premiums. For details contact: Director, Special Markets.

First published in hardcover in 1996 by
Henry Holt and Company, Inc.

First Owl Book Edition—1997

Designed by Victoria Hartman

Printed in the United States of America
All first editions are printed on acid-free paper.∞

1   3   5   7   9   10   8   6   4   2

TO MARY

Contents

III · PATTERNINGS

Acknowledgments

In expressing gratitude, prefer the dry or *pétillant* (slightly sparkling) to the usual treacle.

Treacly

From heart and soul, my thanks to the writer's angels named below. You gave me confidence. You gave me hope. You were there for me. Whatever merits shine through these pages, they reflect the cherished benefit of your talents, generosity, and compassion. Credit my own inadequacies for such errors and follies as remain.

Brut

Abetment of persons involved in the flogging of thoughts into words is an act punishable by acknowledgment. So thank you Sean Morris, linguist; Bruce Frausto, Internet savant; Tom Gaughan, tough-talk consultant; Mary Phelan, artist and critic; Ed Knappman, agent; and Cynthia Vartan, editor-at-large, Henry Holt.

They want to tell each other what they want to tell themselves. But what is bumping like a helium balloon at the ceiling of their brain never finds its way out. It bubbles and rises, it gurgles in the throat, it rolls across the surface of the tongue, and erupts from the lips—a belch.

If they are lucky, there are tears at the end of the long night. . . .

—Sandra Cisneros, "Woman Hollering Creek,"
Woman Hollering Creek and Other Stories

I

Containments

Gasping for Words

*S*omething moves you to express your thoughts. The subject is love. Or beauty. Mortality. Some poignant experience.

You hesitate—and well you should. Launching ideas as messages is not exactly blowing kisses from a train. You are putting thoughts into words, which is more like flapping the tongue to escape gravity. We work our tongues endlessly, but lift-off is so rare it's a miracle we don't keel over like some NASA dud.

Yet we go on flapping rather than fall silent or simply moo at one another. We struggle with words because they separate us from the lowing beasts and tell the world who we are, what we want, and why.

No one will dispute the need for verbal expression, because no one will sit still to listen. The need is assumed, but it is never more clearly illustrated than when Americans visit foreign lands of funny-speaking people. Even with a stock of their funny phrases we find it difficult to express our individuality. We barely distinguish ourselves from the wash jerking on the clotheslines. We feel like babies, unable to express the nuances of pleasure and discontent. And babies hate that feeling.

In foreign travel I often find myself, oh, about fifty thousand words short of being interesting to anyone but the local pickpockets. I remember one moody trip when, traveling alone, I dined night after night talking to my cheeses and such mistakenly ordered dishes as pickled cow's face with hairy nostrils. One evening, a sensitive-looking young couple gestured for me to join them. We exchanged basic phrases, but what I wanted to express was an overflow of feeling, something like this:

> My dear companionable saviors—For the last three weeks a shadow of melancholy has obscured my perceptions, dimming the beauty of your countryside and the conviviality of its inhabitants. Solitude, when no longer self-imposed, soon deepens into isolation and near madness. Now, however, as your kind concern and sensitivity restore my spirit, all that I have perceived unscrolls and engulfs me in its majesty. I exalt in your land and its people.

What came out was the equivalent of "Me like here. Food good. Everything very good. You go America?"

They'd sat a three-year-old at their table.

• • •

It is so often like that, even at home in our native language. We ache for the radiance of expressiveness—of vivid expression. We grope for words to light up the cosmos or the written page or the face across the table. But the harder we try, the more we seem to darken the waters, like a squid in its ink.

This is not a book to scold us squid. We are all in the dark. Only for the most routine messages do our habitual means of expression suffice. We have at hand the words and gestures to convey that it's raining outside, that we feel hung over, that we wish the @#! television turned down. We can describe a head cold ("miserable"), an appliance sale ("unbelievable"), or last night's extra-inning ball game ("great") to our satisfaction. These are generic events, events that perfectly fit a type, and for all anyone cares, we can package them in our most generic language.

Reacting to life's nongeneric stimuli, however, we find ourselves grossly unprepared. So many thoughts and passions stampede inside us, as mad for release as the bulls of Pamplona. But open the gates and see how our puny words scatter, overwhelmed and impotent. We gasp for the telling language and we choke. We rant. We go mute. We claim linguistic fifth amendments: "Words fail me." "It defies description." We buy sympathy cards the size of tombstones just to say, "WORDS CANNOT EXPRESS. . . ."

Let No Gallo Write My Epitaph

Unable to express the nuances of experience, we fall back on generic language in ways that mock our humanity. When wine producer Julio Gallo died in 1993, his brother and sixty-year business partner Ernest offered this statement, according to *The New York Times:*

> Julio was a great brother, a great partner, and a great human being. His passing is a great personal loss to me and both of our families.[1]

Can words no longer express human sentiment? Have our lives grown so subtle and complex as to outrun our 600,000-word heritage? Or has the American experience become such that a few flabby expressions and thirty million handguns say it all?

Perhaps Ernest Gallo was just exhausted, as are most people. Yet even in supercharged moments we succumb to generic drag. Recently three hyperenergetic teens from good schools appeared as guest critics on a television show. Reacting to a remake of the film *Of Mice and Men,* they fairly quivered with insights and jostled for a turn to express them. Yet the expression "Great!" was the sole adjective in their arsenal. Not one of the bright-eyed three could escape the tug of that word.

Each day, even as specialized vocabularies grow, fewer words seem to serve for larger gulps of experience. Every parent knows the tendency of kids to describe the world according to the most fashionable dyad of the day: neat/dumb, excellent/gross, dude/dork, whatever. Millions of adults are already fixated in this stage. At a textbook publishing house in Chicago, for example, one programmer categorizes all phenomena as "cool" or "bummer." Such bipolarity—friend/foe, food/nonfood—smacks of organisms that lick the environment rather than describe it.

But, bummer! Who wants to reverse the miracle of human expression? The more complex our experience, the more we long to unravel it in words. The more generic our lives, the more we yearn to express our individuality. When it comes to language, however, our floundering prompts the saying *"tanto nadar para morir en la orilla"*—so much swimming only to perish at the shore. Twelve, sixteen, twenty years of schooling, inundated by verbiage every day, and we can't speak our hearts.

Generic Patterns

What's the answer? Vocabulary building? That is a partial answer, if one's vocabulary is freshened and not merely encumbered. Hauling around words like *xeric, succedaneum,* or *quaquaversal* can be counterproductive. Word tonnage isn't the point. With no more than eighteen thousand different words, Shakespeare's writings have stimulated the Western world for four centuries; the average American commands some twenty thousand words and about four minutes of attention.

We have lively words, but we are stuck in patterns developed in an age of standardization and mass media. As we parrot standard models that reach for the lowest common denominator, we express ourselves in phrases used by everyone for everything. Often, to compensate for the banality, we pour on pop phrases and jargon like Tabasco over cornflakes. Language to describe distinctive moments or thoughts is parked somewhere in our heads, but the synapses to carry it forward are choked with babble.

"Having an incredible time in the Himalayas," reads a postcard from a young traveler. "The scenery is so excellent. We stayed at some fantastically neat monasteries. The Buddhist-type thing is awesomely mind-boggling and bizarre and could totally change my whole lifestyle. I'm like, where am I?"

A postcard needn't aspire to revelation, but back home its writer will deliver longer versions of these adventures in language no more revealing, even though this traveler has experienced an epiphany of sorts and yearns to describe it. In all areas of expression we find ourselves speaking and writing postcards, stepping back to frame everything in stock generalities and panoramic vistas. And the response we can expect is the one we give to postcards: flip, flop, and into the trash.

Earlier Eloquence

One hears much lamenting about the decline of average language skills in the United States. Sometimes the lamenting itself is lamentable. Comparing writing and speaking skills out of context is slippery business, yet who doesn't marvel at the expressiveness of soldiers, travelers, frontier women, and so many other nonliterary Americans of earlier centuries? Were they better educated? Not necessarily. Were they exposed to superior models? Not always, though perhaps fewer corrupting forces pounded away at them. Were they driven by incentives now meaningless? Perhaps.

Jacob Shallus (1750–96), born in Philadelphia to German-speaking parents, was an ordinary early American I happened to study for a biography I was writing. A clerk and copyist for the Pennsylvania Assembly, he struggled against poverty yet aspired to the lofty style of the documents he inscribed on parchment (including the Constitution of the United States). In 1788, even as he groveled for a loan, he groveled eloquently. Imagine Visa receiving this note:

> Sir
> Being arrested for the sum of Twelve pounds some odd shillings and likely to be under the necessity of going to confinement, I have taken the freedom to address you for my relief as well as that of a wife and eight children who must otherwise feel the effects of my situation—Good Sir I can restore it to you as soon as the Assembly meet, therefore intreat you will estend your friendship to a person altho' little known to you but who will exert himself upon every occasion for your Service. Pray do not deny me and contemplate that you are lending a small pittance for a few days only and thereby destroy the violent intentions of an unrelenting Creditor.
> I am,
> Sir   With great esteem
>   Your very hble serv.
>   JShallus

Not masterly prose or contemporary spelling, but how many civil servants today can toss off these elegant constructions? Before democratization softened class distinctions, a pretty way with words affirmed one's status, helped separate one from the lower orders. Conversely, low-born citizens might mask or even transcend their origins by imitating the diction of the elevated.

Today, however, we speak as blandly or as jargony as we please; we speak the language of our subcultures, and, hey, whoever don't like it can you-know-what. Recently I saw a T-shirt that proclaimed, IF YOU DON'T LIKE MY ATTITUDE, STOP TALKING TO ME! Status rarely drives us to acquire a more "cultured" or more generally expressive idiom. English teachers may point us toward "prescriptive" grammar, that is, the "standard" patterns used by the society's leading white literati, but substandard grammar won't bar us from Martha's Vineyard, a skybox at the Super Bowl, or even the boardroom. Americans judge status by many factors other than expression. Too often one hears, "How much does that SOB *make* to be opening his mouth?" and not always, "His stunning way with words assures us of his authority."

Still, the longing for expressiveness remains, if not to achieve status then to experience the joy and relief of getting what's inside outside. Unexpressed, the particular richness of a life is lost in the mall of generic memory. We barely know what an experience was until we shape it into words that somehow distinguish it. Sensing this, most of us have resolved to sharpen our powers of expression, just as we've resolved to firm up those hips and thighs; but a thousand obstacles slow us down. We tend toward inertia; we need prodding.

Cyrano de Plotnik

Prodding, of course, can be gentle or otherwise. The most classic example of "otherwise" occurs in Edmond Rostand's drama *Cyrano de Bergerac,* when the swashbuckling Cyrano tutors an enemy aristocrat in expressiveness.

Having disrupted a theater performance, Cyrano offers "pointed" appreciation to anyone in the audience who will describe, as a subject of comedy, his famous, prodigious nose.

The Viscount de Valvert steps forward. "Your nose is big, very large," he sputters.

Working the crowd, Cyrano responds (in rhymed French): "That's it? Rather brief, young man. Oh! God! There are so many ways you might have expressed it!"

Cyrano then offers the lesson, challenging himself to invent a pithy insult of his nose in each of nineteen categories, including pedantic, eloquent, dramatic, admiring, lyric, rustic, military, and practical. For example:

Dramatic: 'Tis the Red Sea when it Bleeds!
Admiring: The very sign a perfume shop needs!

And so on, in a panoply of self-insult that Cyrano now turns on Valvert—"These, Sir Idiot, are things you might have said, had you some tinge of letters, or wit, within your head." With that, the swords are drawn. Even as they duel, Cyrano describes the swordplay in an extemporaneous ballad, speeding to the immortal line:

Then, as I end the refrain . . . thrust home!

The viscount falls, the wiser in matters of expression—but unfortunately, run through.

•   •   •

Now, that's prodding. But there is also the gentler sort. Enter this book and its author, your very hble serv., APlotnik. Who is APlotnik? On the one hand, I am a career observer of expression, awash in credentials as an author, editor, publisher, and speaker. On the other hand, I remain a struggler after expressiveness, a stumbler, someone who still bleeds over every sentence, pounds tables and slams doors at the frustration of trying to express the most elemental thought. I am as guilty of small talk as any hairdresser and not unknown to say "Great!" and "Really!" in the process. Thus there will be no superior tone, no linguistic snobbery, here. In fact, some passages—maybe this one—will be monuments to the peril of opening one's yap.

It should come easier to me. As a younger man I lived and worked in New York City, where snappy expressiveness is the *sine qua non* of getting attention, where even failure to articulate a sandwich order can mean shame and lost opportunity. But when the formidable delicatessen clerks cried "Next!" I was often the hesitator, the one who lost his turn as he drawled, "Let me think. . . ."

I'm still thinking. Not only about the power of expression to secure an onion bagel lightly toasted Nova lox no butter with a schmear (of cream cheese)—but beyond! My thinking about expression, as I observe our ways with words, informs this little book. Although I've tried to pick up where the often-stern *Elements of Style* (William Strunk and E. B. White) leaves off, this is no pedantic treatise. I've written *The Elements of Expression* to give pleasure, drawing on all levels of expressiveness. Along the way, however, it might prod you to think about language; to break out of generic patterns; to choose more expressive words from known and near-known vocabularies; and to arrange words in more stimulating ways.

If all that feels a bit dry, then simply enjoy the fun of lively expression as we explore it. Not to take anything away from water rifles and computer games, but words—sacred, silly, or profane—still provide some of the best diversion that life has to offer.

2

Standard English:
Who Needs It?

*D*oes good expression mean mastery of "Standard" English? What is Standard English, anyway? And where's the fun in it?

You want fun? Watch how language authorities sweat when they try to define Standard English. See how they grope for terms that are not biased toward their own heritage. Standard English, many authorities say, is the language of "educated people." But educated in what? Educated by whom? Are we talking about Ivy Leaguers or grease monkey–*savants*?

Virtually all the common definitions are biased: Standard English is "elegant" English. (Elegant to whom?) The English of "the prestige members of a community." Of "people who read a great deal . . . bookish people." "Proper or official English." "Cultivated English." "The consensus of influential people." "The language of good manners." One definition, "the spoken and written English of mature, socially responsible . . . adults," bars some of my best friends from the club.

Oh, we know what these definitions mean, more or less; that certain cultural leaders set a standard the rest of us recognize, even if grudgingly. But who exactly are these coxswains of the language?

Now watch me sweat as I try to explain.

People of the Word

Most societies harbor a subculture best described as the word people. These are the people who think about words and who take pains to express themselves clearly, logically, and in a civil manner. Whatever they are called—intelligentsia, linguists, literati, control freaks, elders—they are people who have won the respect of the education and literary establishments. The word people set a standard for "respectable" expression when they speak or write for the public.

The preferred words and word patterns of these respected people are collected by the subculture's word keepers. The keepers, word people themselves, are known as language authorities. They preserve and categorize the preferred language in dictionaries, grammars, usage guides, and other texts.

The authorities look also to the past. They consider how the language was used by certain favored writers and described by earlier authorities. Many of these older patterns, they say, still function splendidly among word people; ergo, these patterns along with approved new ones constitute a standard.

The more enduring standard patterns are often expressed as "rules." The rules help people use words in consistent, recognizable ways. These words and patterns, say the authorities, constitute "standard" or "formal written English." The most consistent application of Standard English and its rules occurs in published English; that is, in reputable or mainstream published English, not the flyers from the pizza joint.

Compared to spoken English, the published word attains greater distribution, authority, and longevity; it calls for exacting care. The published word must stand up to scrutiny and deliver its intended meaning to broad audiences over extended times. Even tabloids must use recognizable, standard patterns in describing the two-headed baby born of Elvis and a Venusian. Tabloids aside, published English is sometimes called "edited English," meaning there is a more fastidious adherence to rules than with the standard spoken word.

Regulators and Guardians

Sometimes a society assigns its language-regulating function to a government agency, such as France's Académie Française, established in 1635. However, no such agencies have survived for English, a great drifting sponge of a language. Some of the English-language keepers, fearing chaos, have appointed themselves regulators and guardians. Their mission: to strengthen the standard around which responsible users of the language can regroup, fend off corruption, and monitor change. Standard American English has come by way of such regulators, both Brits and Yanks, including H. W. and F. G. Fowler, Sir Ernest Gowers, Wilson Follett, H. L. Mencken, Margaret M. Bryant, Theodore Bernstein, Bergen and Cornelia Evans, Jacques Barzun, and E. B. White.

Such language guardians are worthy people, even when driven by egos the size of *Webster's* unabridged. They are heroes. Their teeth ache, the freethinkers mock them, their children rebel. Undeterred, they fight for precision in the language. They will argue with mind-boggling tenacity, for example, that *boggle* is an intransitive verb and therefore incapable of transmitting action from subject to object. The mind can boggle at something, but nothing can boggle the mind. So there.

The most intractable of these guardians are called "prescriptive," because they prescribe what people *ought* to say to be counted among the world's gentility. Prescriptivists divide expression into "right" and "wrong." If they are slow to accept change, they are called "purists."

Other language keepers call themselves *"descriptive,"* merely recording words and their uses without making value judgments. The purist-prescriptivists consider descriptivists the scourge of civilization. Yet even descriptive authorities concede that a language, at least in its written form, needs a framework of conventions to link users across subcultures and time periods. Otherwise a language fast becomes a sea of sub-lingos, impossible to navigate. Imagine a vocabulary without rules, even for punctuation:

> "Vamoose me shall,?, split' like feel I had'!?"
> "rappin sorry to was yang yin you:; youse I."
> "supersimpatico . . . not be will to us'n—,."

With a body of shared or standard word patterns, however, people can exchange clear meanings and subtle thoughts, perhaps stimulate one another.

> "I should be going. I feel as if I've already gone."
> "I'm sorry, were you speaking to me?"
> "I'm not sure. Shall we become acquainted?"

Rules offer a framework for communication, but they guarantee neither clarity nor force. Standard English can also accommodate the stupefying and excessive.

> "Well, I suppose one should be going, seeing that one seems to have been both perceptibly and irrevocably gone."
> "Would that I knew the intent of she who so bewitchingly calls forth."
> "Having spoken to you without having had the least notion of one's own intent, one would not be averse to discouraging an incipient misunderstanding."

Getting Standardized

Standard English, well employed, is a roomy, consistent, clever framework for intelligent expression. Whoops—"clever" and "intelligent" are hopelessly subjective. Never mind. We are not saying Standard English is the *only* framework for brainy expression, just a very successful one. No normal person uses it in all situations. Better patterns pop up for use in traffic brawls, barroom banter, pillow talk, and in all sorts of spoken and written exchanges. In fact, part of the fun of Standard English is to abuse it in ways that create excitement and aesthetic tension. But first one must master enough Standard English to have a basis for abuse.

If only from patterns heard on the airwaves, most people absorb some sense of the standard. But it is another matter to master the more complex structures and subtle nuances of the written language and even a twentieth of the Standard English vocabulary. To walk among the word people is a choice and long-term commitment. It is not everyone's first priority. Millions of Americans ain't got no truck with no authorities when they choose they blankety-blank words.

Yet standardized communications allow people to tie into power structures, rather than merely signal basic needs. Consider how computers would spark and sputter in our faces without the standardized "languages" and "protocols" we design for them. Sputtering people are even more dangerous; the wrong sputter on a street corner can be fatal. But while computers can be programmed in a couple of jolts, people plug into thousands of circuits before they power up as talking machines capable of standard and nonstandard modes. One typical sequence:

Imitating how Mommy and Daddy speak
Imitating how bad Uncle Frank speaks
Suffering through Ms. Thistlebottom's grammar classes
Writing to pen pals
Sorting out television English
Fumbling for self-expression with friends
Lip-synching pop lyrics
Learning Bible and other formal verse
Awakening to high-school literature

Writing papers
Imitating professors and admired peers in college
Surviving Professor Stickler's dreaded composition course
Using language-reference works
Memorizing great love poems
Adventuring among "lowlife"
Reading writers of different backgrounds, different periods
Writing poetry
Watching Spike Lee films
Acting Shakespeare
Writing job application letters
Writing business correspondence
Speaking at banquets
Traveling the world
Teaching the language
Learning new patterns, and unlearning those that no
    longer work

Thus programmed, an individual can articulate thoughts in Standard English when appropriate, or come up with other patterns for other situations.

Generic and High-Flown Standard English

Ever eager to be liked, Americans often play the chameleon and mimic distinctive speech characteristics of their audience. "Splendid to see you." "What's happenin', baby?" For their own standard voice, however, most Americans embrace Brand-X English, the least adventurous—the voice of mass communications. This generic version of Standard English rolls from our lips before we pause to shape a thought. One level fits all. The same version creeps into our writing and spreads like kudzu ivy.

Standard generic is the English we use for routine communication, with relatively minor variations in word choice and pattern as situations change. Is it serviceable? Fairly so. Is it expressive? Hardly. It is a bland abridgment of Standard English, the low end. It is the robotic spiel of flight attendants: "For your safety and convenience, we ask that you refrain from moving about the cabin. . . ." It is the language of corporate statements, voice mail, sound bites. When athletes say, "It was a team victory; every one of us gave one hundred and ten percent," they are speaking one hundred percent standard generic English at a stimulation level of one-half percent.

The highly structured, vocabulary-rich English that underlies "sophisticated" literature might be considered the high end of Standard English. Rare in spoken communications, it is sometimes called "choice written English." Such authors as John Updike, Vladimir Nabokov, Susan Sontag, and V. S. Naipaul are virtuosos of the form. It is not necessarily a florid style, but one characterized by meticulous, nongeneric word choice and seamless flow.

Many language authorities campaign for the "simple and direct" in Standard English, both written and spoken. This is an engaging area into which we will later stick a toe. In spoken literary English, however, Americans seem to admire a dressier standard, one that Alistair Cooke helped propagate every Sunday evening as host of *Masterpiece Theater*—"It was to have been the penultimate adventure from which Sir Richard would emerge unscathed." The locutions of the Mother Tongue still charm us. "How goes it, my lady?" "Ah, one is not as well as one would wish."

We like old-time resonance, too, in the language of high ceremony: "Let each young graduate sally forth, to forge, upon the anvil of destiny, the sword of hope. . . ." Obviously this high-flown standard can become as predictable, as generic, as Brand-X English. Good writers mix high and low for the most original effects. William Faulkner closed his 1950 Nobel acceptance speech, on humankind's redemption through language, with these words:

> When the last ding-dong of doom has clanged and faded from the last worthless rock hanging tideless in the last red and dying evening, . . . even then there will still be one more sound: that of his [man's] puny, inexhaustible voice, still talking.

Such is the English we might aspire to if we wish to stimulate certain highbrow audiences and be known for our "eloquence" of expression. We needn't have it under control every minute, thank God.

Ranking the Nonstandard

Authorities have not only divided Standard English into formal and less formal levels, but have tried to create a ladder of nonstandard English patterns. The rungs have been designated as colloquial, slang, cant, jargon, argot, dialect, and taboo or vulgar; also, vernacular, provincial, regional, illiterate, and so on.

These nonstandard levels were once assigned social rank, ranging from the equivalent of a tolerable merchant class to the lowest or "substandard" untouchable. Some authorities still use the hierarchical designations, but between choice written English and the basest grunts at ringside, there are so many mixed patterns and so many shifts in usage that some authorities have despaired of drawing clear boundaries. Instead they observe the situational use of a term (e.g., "an endearment between intimates") and its effect ("considered offensive to some women"), without assigning status.

In 1961, *Webster's Third New International Dictionary* broke with the tradition of the earlier Merriam-Webster International editions, which had served as authorities on "standard" or "correct" usage. The Third Edition described words in common use, included a great range of uses, and shunned usage labels and notes that would elevate one class of user over another. When it chose to use a status label for certain controversial utterances, it was lenient; for example, it classified *irregardless* as "nonstandard," considering it "too widely current in reputable context to be labeled *substand.*" It allowed that *ain't* is "used orally in most parts of the U.S. by many cultivated speakers." The Second Edition had called the word *illit.*

Webster's Third threw open the door to relative measures of "correctness." The prescriptivists were livid. How dare this trusted authority abrogate its responsibility, no longer distinguishing between right and wrong! "Scientific revolution," steamed Dwight Macdonald in a published critique of the dictionary, "has meshed gears with a trend toward permissiveness, in the name of democracy, that is debasing our language by rendering it less precise. . . ."

Descriptivists, of course, cheered editor Philip Gove's stand against what he considered elitism. The old war heated up: Linguistic conservatives and liberals, the pure and the permissive, were at each other's throats. The fun continues today as we seek to do the "correct" thing in our way with words.

3

Grammar and Other Night Sweats

*I*s Standard English the same as "correct" English?

Not always. "Correct English is English that goes off well in the situation in which it is used," declared Paul Roberts decades ago in a grammar text.[1] And Paul baby, you said a mouthful.

As an undergraduate I read Roberts's advice but soon buried it along with the scores of grammatical fine points to which English majors are exposed. In the ensuing years I would see that different audiences call for various levels of speech, yet I would think of only one level as being "correct"—that divine level once revealed to me, and now, for my sins, removed from memory. I suffered a mild case of what some call "language anxiety."

So heed these words: "Correct" depends upon your audience. Are you writing for the nitpicking readership of *Verbatim: The Language Quarterly,* or telephoning Vito Popovici at the truck-parts warehouse? Here's a quiz no one should fail:

Choose the correct English for stimulating Mr. Popovici:
(a) "I should be most favorably inclined toward your expeditious delivery of the transmission heretofore discussed, as

no little time has passed since your having received my pre-
mature remittance."

(b) "Yo, Vito—you gonna send the #@! gears or what?"

The notion of "correct" English as a measure of grace or
high breeding has given rise to The Shame of Incorrectness.
Shame haunts the study and practice of English expression. It
looms in the shadows like a lunatic professor—the homicidal
Dr. Wrong! Hideously disfigured in his youth by a split infini-
tive, *Dr. Wrong!* now stalks the grammatically weak with his steel
pointer, shrieking *"Wrong!"* as he drives the weapon home.
Bringer of night sweats, he has darkened every academic approach to expression, including grammar, usage, style, and
rhetoric.

But *Dr. Wrong!*—you are banned from this classroom. Out,
shame! In, light! As we confront the real nemesis of expression—Dr. Generic—we might find the old bugaboos to be
friends-in-need. Let's take a look:

Grammar

Linguist Noam Chomsky has defined grammar as "a device of
some sort" for producing a language's sentences. Grammarians study various levels of expression to see how parts of
speech come together to produce a sentence. They then categorize and name the parts—plural subject, transitive verb, direct object, etc.—and describe their functions.

Even our odd twists of expression have names and places in
a grammar system. For example, we've all heard of prefixes
and suffixes, but what do we call the part "bloody" when we
scream, "I'm sick of your homeobloodypathic cures"? It is an
infix, an element attached inside the body of its host.

What puts most people off about grammar are the hordes of
impossible-to-remember names and functions often based on
Latin and Latin structure, along with the notion that we *have* to

remember them or be shamed. We certainly don't have to; we can imitate and embellish the forms we admire without knowing their classifications. But grammar sources (see also "Usage," below) help steer our choices, and, like caring mentors, put things in perspective.

Suppose you were writing a letter to *The New York Review of Books* that began, "I want to tell it like it is." Should you have said "*as* it is"? A grammar source recommends the use of "as" for a literate audience and offers a rationale:

> Adverb clauses of manner answer the question *how?* The principal conjunctions are *as, as if, as though, in that.*
> [example] I write *as I please.* . . .
> *Like* and *how* are sometimes used to introduce clauses of manner, but not in Choice English:
> [non-Choice example] Do it *like I told you.*[2]

You might still prefer the idiomatic "tell it like it is" for this "clause of manner," but now at least you know the more formal, or "choice written," pattern.

True descriptive grammar loves all its children, from educated Choice to urchin Vulgate; it tries not to favor one kid as more "correct" than another. Yet most books of grammar focus on choice English, so that the patterns of the so-called educated class are perceived as the rules of "correctness." But as we've said, it ain't necessarily so.

How much fun can grammar be? Many have approached it lightheartedly, including William Safire in his paradoxical "Fumblerules"—e.g., "Don't use no double negatives." Karen Elizabeth Gordon puts a Gothic twist on grammar lessons in *The Transitive Vampire* and similar works (see Resources). But students will probably never find much entertainment in grammar except to snicker at such terms as *loose apposition* and *copulative verb*.

Too many grammatical concepts carry the baggage of classical Greek, Latin, and eighteenth- and nineteenth-century pedantry. A bout with "tense relationships of the modal auxiliaries" weighs as heavy on the brain as the phrase on the tongue. The important thing to know is that word people have developed an operation-and-repair manual for Standard English. When we need to fine-tune our expression to a literate audience, grammar is a system and a source we can rely on.

But for all the attempts at making it fun, grammar remains a sophisticated discipline whose true masters are mainly scholars. Certain schemes place within grammar the fields of *syntax* (the study of word relationships in a sentence), *phonology* (study of language sounds), and *semantics* (study of linguistic meaning). Otto Jespersen's *A Modern English Grammar on Historical Principles* (1909–31) fills seven volumes, and *A Comprehensive Grammar of the English Language* by Randolph Quirk et al. runs to 1,779 pages. Obviously some people have a passion for unraveling complexities or interrelating abstract concepts in a logical system. Such people will carry on the noble science of grammar. The rest of us need big drawings of gears and pulleys before we turn our attention to how things work.

Usage

Grammar describes *general* patterns in the language; for example, "Plural verb forms are used with plural subjects."

Usage tracks *particular* patterns in contemporary expression. A usage note might read:

> Many American writers use the Latin plural *data* with a singular verb form, e.g., "the data yields no sign of intelligent life in Washington."

Grammar and usage intertwine. Grammatical patterns influence use of words, and use of words eventually establishes broader patterns. But usage changes infinitely faster than grammar—as fast as millions of language users strive for originality, as fast as new uses bubble up in the mass media and electronic networks. Published grammars can take years to integrate usage into a system, but dictionaries and usage guides such as the *Harper Dictionary of Contemporary Usage* are frequently updated. Electronic publishing will probably force more updates than anyone wants.

Language journals and columnists offer the latest in word fashion, which is more or less what usage amounts to. Usage is a gossipy record of What the Who's Who Are Wearing in Words. Prescriptive authorities consider upper-crust fashions to be "correct" usage. The descriptive camp says, "We're hanging it all on the rack, kiddo. Pick it out as needed."

Usage guides come in all flavors: prescriptive, descriptive, and mixed. The prescriptive *Modern American Usage* (by Wilson Follett, completed by Jacques Barzun) says, in effect: "Look, Dunce, this is how the terms are used by people who count, so pay attention." For example, on the persistent question of *like* and *as*, the guide advises:

> Comparisons involving a verb are introduced by *as* or *as if,* not by *like.* . . . *Like* is now even more repellent when it means *as if* than when it means simply *as,* and it becomes intolerable when it is used with calculated archness by those who know better: *Wartime Italy demanded opera like wartime America demands movies.* [Incorrect.]

One is tempted to respond, "We need your contemptuous tone as we need a hole in the head." However, measuring ourselves against the self-assured can be instructive. The Folletts, Fowlers, and other language regulators present a rationale for most of their choices. That rationale, at least, provides a basis for argument and change.

Recognizing that self-assuredness takes many forms, some usage guides strive for consensus among groups of word people. "The days when one person . . . [can] dictate the rights and wrongs of language are long gone," said editors William and Mary Morris when their *Harper Dictionary of American Usage* first appeared in 1975. The Morrises created a "usage panel" of some 136 writers, editors, and public speakers who in the Morrises' view used the language "carefully and effectively." (Panels had been in use for decades; *The American Heritage Dictionary* under William Morris assembled one in the mid-sixties.)

The Harper panel, a mix of types ranging from cartoonist Walt Kelly to Harvard President Emeritus James B. Conant, offered opinions on scores of problematic words and phrases. The Morrises then tallied these opinions into percentages in favor and against.

On the *like/as* question, for example, twelve percent of the panel favored using the preposition *like* also as a conjunction (e.g., "Winston tastes good like a cigarette should"). For casual speech, such use was approved by twenty-eight percent.

In another vote, sixty percent approved use of the word *uptight* as a synonym for "tense" in casual conversation. Only twenty percent said they used it in their own writing. From today's perspective, the 1975 panel—which was anything but multicultural—seems rather uptight itself, fussing over what it considered permissible written English. But it did help loosen the dictates of the most prescriptive grammarians. The panel was asked: Can "whose" be used in reference to animals, as in "the dog *whose* collar was lost"? About three-fourths of the panelists said yes, one noting, "I'm for the dog every time!"

Style

In written communications, *style* is a term with two principal meanings that are sometimes confused. The first refers to a body of detailed mechanical rules and guidelines for presenting a piece of writing; for example, the Associated Press style for reporters, Modern Language Association style for scholars, and *The Chicago Manual of Style* for editors. Style guides assure that presentations for a given audience will be consistent in their mechanics. The major guides cover a dizzying range of detail, from arrangement of footnotes to preferences in capitalization and spelling out numbers. Some go beyond mere mechanics, advising, for example, how to avoid sex-specific terms such as *postman*. Others offer guidance on terms preferred within a certain field. For journalists, *The Washington Post Deskbook on Style* (1st ed., 1978) notes that "A man **dies** and is **buried** in a **coffin** by an **undertaker** or **funeral director;** he does not **pass away** and is not **interred** in a **casket** by a **mortician.**" But most mechanical-style guides influence expression only indirectly, assisting in questions of form.

Style in its second sense, however, means everything that makes expression distinctive. If grammar is the skeleton of expression and usage the flesh and blood, then style is the personality. Thomas S. Kane, in *The New Oxford Guide to Writing* (1988), calls style "the total of all the choices a writer makes concerning words and their arrangements." It is not, he says, "a superficial fanciness brushed over the basic ideas," but "the deep essence of writing."

Elsewhere in this book we address style—in spoken as well as written expression—and some of the choices that shape it. And the shapes one finds! From plain to florid, lean to voluptuous, mannered to manic. We'll visit the major types and a few weirdos.

Rhetoric

In its broad contemporary sense, *rhetoric* means the art of writing well—expressively and persuasively. A contrary meaning as in "Give me facts, not rhetoric!" may be more familiar; for centuries rhetoric was, in part, the science of seducing an audience by art and artifice in expression. Spoken rhetoric is traditionally called oratory, and most of today's artful orators are involved in one seduction or another. Thus rhetoric carries its negative connotation of bombast along with its meaning as the art of effective communication.

Techniques of modern prose are rarely taught as "rhetoric" per se; but "composition" and creative writing courses reflect the twenty-five-century history of rhetoric as a core educational system. Rhetoric flowered in ancient Greece as the art of oratory, aiming at clarity, impressiveness, decorum, beauty, and purity of language. Approaches ranged from the plain style to the highly mannered with its colorful devices—epithets, antitheses, rhythm, and rhymed endings. Elevated by the genius of Cicero, rhetoric applied itself to all types of discourse over the centuries, including persuasive argument in law. Always the study of rhetoric was organized into lists, classifications, and elements, such as:

- Threefold aim: to instruct, to move, and to delight
- Five steps to successful composition: invention, disposition, style (elocution), memory, delivery
- Chief instrument of delight: style
- Four virtues of style: correctness, clarity, elegance, and appropriateness

And so on. The figures of speech taught today, such as *metaphor, paradox,* and *simile,* are but a handful of the several hundred "rhetorical figures" introduced as elements of style by classical rhetoricians. *Eulogia* is among the few classical elements of "emotional appeal" still recognized by name. Not many Americans know they express an act of *paramythia* in sending a sympathy card, or of *bdelygmia* in crying "Yuk!"

The Renaissance saw the birth of humanist rhetoric, with its dictionaries, textbooks, and memorization procedures for imitating classical models of expression. Along with grammar and logic, rhetoric had long formed a *trivium* within the seven-part "fallacy" system of formal education. Rhetoric taught how to use the linguistic structure (grammar) with power and grace. Its purpose was elegance and persuasiveness, but not necessarily truth. Truth was the business of logic.

In the sixteenth century rhetoric concerned itself more with delivery than content and began to decline as an organizing educational principle. By the nineteenth century certain educators condemned organized rhetorical study; they called classical interest in rhetoric "a monstrous aberration."

Though the formal discipline declined, the term survived among teachers of writing and speaking. In the twentieth century it enjoyed a revival, aided in part by I. A. Richards's *Philosophy of Rhetoric* (1941), which called for a new art of discourse and influenced teaching in schools and universities. "Rhetoric" reappeared in titles of texts, such as *Modern Rhetoric* by Cleanth Brooks and Robert Penn Warren (1st ed., 1949); academics studying aspects of effective use of language embraced rhetoric as an umbrella term and used it to lend prestige to such treatises as *The Transformational Density of Dickinson's Rhetoric*.[3]

Today's mass-market publishers may shy from the term as antiquated and onerous-sounding. William Zinsser's popular *On Writing Well* is a "rhetoric" for students that dares not say so. But it does say this: Good writers "are vastly dissimilar in style and personality, but they have all learned the one lesson that must be learned: how to control their material." Rhetoricians would agree.

The New Arbiters

As on most matters, society swings back and forth on the question of language control. Are we to encourage dynamism and diversity in mainstream expression or embrace the comforting "purity, propriety, and precision" first preached by Lindley Murray in his 1794 *English Grammar*? What is to be our measure of correctness in written communications?

Consider today's environment, a rock concert–like din of overloaded and understimulated brains. Today, when an audience pays the extraordinary price of its attention, it wants recognizable or standard patterns, yes. But that's only the beginning. To compete with other stimuli, written expression had better deliver relevance! Payoff! Utility! Information! Transformation! Feedback! Power! Control!

In the last few decades we have seen the rise of, among other phenomena, New Journalism and its rude vitality; instantaneous electronic feedback; the demands of a culturally diverse audience; and the not-always-deplorable expectation of entertainment as a reward for attention. In this environment, individual expression calls for an aggressiveness, an exuberance, a responsiveness—most of which traditional handbooks of style pass by.

No single arbiter or printed authority can keep up with new influences on a nation's forms of expression. Perhaps the closest to a handbook for the masses has been *The Elements of Style* by William Strunk, Jr., and E. B. White, a best-seller since its appearance in 1959. But even when new editions update its selected rules, some of the advice remains musty. Try achieving force, originality, or texture under these Strunk and White restrictions: *Do not inject opinion. Use figures of speech sparingly. Place yourself in the background. Do not affect a breezy manner. Avoid foreign language. Prefer the standard to the offbeat.*

Some recent handbooks recognize the limitations of standard patterns even as they teach them (see Resources). But a true "authority" for the masses today would be something like "Strunk, White, Brown, Paz, Quinn, Wang, Sato, Szydlowski, and Sitting Bear"—an electronic handbook on-line to every writer, updated daily, with chapters by a rotating rainbow coalition of our most expressive language users, people who chew up Standard English and spew it out in a blizzard of confetti cheered by the multitudes.

II

Extrusions

Expressiveness

*E*xpressiveness is the goal. Expression is what we use to get there.

Dictionaries like to define the word *expressive* as "full of expression." What an alluring image! Of all the things we could be full of, expression may be one of the most delectable. Yet not every stuffing is savory. Expression includes anything—form, phrase, pose, costume, etc.—that manifests a thought, feeling, or quality.[1] Such manifestations cover about 97 percent of organic behavior, from the sublime to the icky.

Mooning from a dormitory window is expression. So, too, is what naturalist Adrian Forsyth describes as "the facial grimace and the clutching and reaching reaction of a female stump-tailed macaque" as it mates. Hot-oil wrestling is expression. Michael Jackson's moonwalk. A slam dunk. A backward baseball cap. Telemarketing. Elevator talk. And so on. All forms of expression, some expressive, some not.

Expressiveness is an onslaught of stimulation that seizes and engages an audience. In observing communication between organisms, behavioral scientists use the term *arousal* for responses involving alertness to stimuli. But arousal has become too sexy a word for general use here. *Engagement* is the better term. Most readers of this book seek to engage an audience of sensitive humans. Why? To transmit knowledge, dazzle a loved one, impress an editor, close a deal, get a laugh, or share anguish, among a zillion other motives. Whatever its mission, however, the arc sent out to crackle in someone else's brain usually encounters some resistance. Expressive power drives it home.

Words Rule

Of all means of expression available to our species—word, gesture, sign, image, melody, aroma, bite—words constitute the most complete system of communicating ideas and emotions. Inadequate as words often seem, they rule expressiveness.

Painters, musicians, and other nonliterary artists are vigorous purveyors of words even as they claim to speak through their art. Both they and their audiences tend to reach beyond the works themselves for meanings that connect minds and hearts. They reach for the power of words.

Van Gogh pushed visual expression to the outer limits, yet his concepts seemed to outrace what he could express in painting. In addition to haranguing friends over coffees and absinthes, he verbalized his thoughts in volumes of now-famous correspondence. He used words profusely, sometimes clumsily, sometimes soppily, but ultimately in ways "full of expression."

> . . . I am always between two currents of thought, first the material difficulties, turning round and round to make a living; and second, the study of color. I am always in hope of making a discovery there, to express the love of two lovers by a wedding of two complementary colors, their mingling and their opposition, the mysterious vibrations of kindred tones. To express the thought of a brow by the radiance of a light tone against a somber background.
>
> To express hope by some star, the eagerness of a soul by a sunset radiance. Certainly there is no delusive realism in that. . . .[2]

Words such as these (written from Arles in 1888, two years before his death, to his brother Theo) helped engage critics, biographers, novelists, and film producers—and thus an audience of millions—in the passions of an artist whose works engaged so few in his time.

Nonverbal Expression

Words rule the empire of expressiveness, and words will be our focus. We will not, however, overlook the power of nonverbal expression to stimulate response. How could we? Since Darwin called attention to body language in *The Expression of the Emotions in Man and Animal* (1872), researchers are said to have identified some one million nonverbal clues and signals.

Nonverbal language includes not just squirms and gestures, but tone of voice, puffs, whistles, raspberries (Bronx cheers), and such vocalized nonwords *(segregates)* as the "mm" response to somebody's troubles or "mm-*mm!*" over a plate of steaming gumbo. According to one observer, certain Arabs "sometimes stand close enough to use the quality of each other's breath as an important and personal source of information."[3] In all, nonverbal language often accounts for more than half the number of interpersonal messages we communicate, say studies of such matters.

Whole nations specialize in expressive gestures. In India, the *mudras,* or symbolic hand gestures, are revered as one of the elements linking the human world with its divine counterpart. Classical dancers combine *mudras* with other expressions—particularly of the eyes—to evoke vivid imagery. As the ritual verses describe it:

> Where the hand goes, the eye must go,
> Where the eyes go, the mind goes,
> Where the mind, there the expression,
> Where there is expression, there is joy.

Expression illustrated. A century ago recitation texts offered drawings of "the typical and most important gestures" for conveying various attitudes and emotions. "The body," one text advised, "with voice, eyes, hands, arms, head, in short, with all its members that were made to talk, should express the exact thought and sentiment of the reading." The advice and the drawings shown are from *The Model Orator*, edited by Henry Davenport Northrop (Chicago: A. B. Kuhlman, 1895).

Florid hand gestures extend into everyday Indian life. Elsewhere other body movements prevail. Japan with its bows. Italy with its language of fingers, chins, and elbows. Yanks may come up short in the elbows department, but they have their own specialties. High-fives and after-touchdown shuffles seem to have been perfected on U.S. playing fields. To symbolize a grown-up's stupidity, the American eight-year-old displays a patented combination of puckered mouth and furrowed brow—an expression that turns parents into psychic rubble.

Most face-making is expressive. Think of comedian Billy Crystal's pinched features or ex-tackle Mike Singletary's narrowed eyes. Facial poses are aptly called expressions. "Wipe that expression off your face!" we tell the brat. Actors study facial expression. Writers must devise means for conveying it in words:

"[The Swiss waiter] looked as if he had just learned that his wife had run off with the milkman and taken all his Waylon Jennings albums." (Bill Bryson, *Neither Here nor There*, Avon, 1992)

What's So Difficult?

Expressiveness or vivid expression may seem no big mystery to those who consider themselves animated. Just lean into the audience, flutter the hands, bounce the eyebrows, and talk in loud bursts like Joan Rivers or the brothers Click and Clack. Or look *intense*, like Bill Moyers interviewing Joseph Campbell. These techniques may work at first, astonishing friends who see you acting so bizarre. But with no substance behind them, no humor, art, or intelligence, such mannerisms soon become ordinary and even irksome.

Beginning writers look for easy expressiveness. They pull modifiers off the racks—"With a haughty toss of her curls, she laughed scornfully, rebelliously." They pour on the CAPS, *italics*, and *exclamations!* They uncork the obvious, denying readers the pleasure of completing a suggested thought. They favor language a size too large for the substance at hand. Even Virgil was criticized (by A. F. Housman) for "the besetting sin" of using words "too forcible for his thoughts." Sometimes would-be writers mistake the frequent use of "expressions"—familiar word groupings, clichés—for expressiveness. Clichés are once-stimulating phrases dulled by their very popularity. As critic John Simon notes, " 'Vanity of a peacock' is to imagery what a twenty-times-used razor blade is to shaving" *(Paradigms Lost).*

Expressiveness may come easily enough at odd moments. We have all been surprised by a show-stopping remark from some drunken dullard (perhaps oneself). The class dunce writes an inspired line of poetry. The jock turns a clever phrase. Even a murderous robot named Terminator finds *"Hasta la vista, baby!"* in its program of one-liners, launching an international catchphrase. When sufficiently angered, we can all work up a version of saliva-dripping rage to get attention. But how many of us can write three pages that sustain interest? Or engage an audience as we retell a movie plot, a comedy sketch, a problem at work? Do we ordinarily rivet our audience, or do we inspire that *"hasta la vista"* look in their eyes?

The Art of Extrusion

There are cheap and easy ways to grab a minute's attention. The bearer of the latest dirt at the office can't miss. But at any sustained level expressiveness is an art, especially for the demanding audiences we court. It is not easy. It was never meant to be.

Consider the etymology of the verb *express;* it derives from *expressare,* a form of the Medieval Latin *exprimere (ex-*out, *premere,* to press, push). In early usage *express* meant not only to depict, but "to press out" or "form by pressure." *Expressive,* before the fifteenth century, meant tending to press out or expel.[4] That sense of pressing and pushing, although lost in modern usage, characterizes the art of extruding meanings or of forming messages.

Expressiveness is not limited to formally trained artists nor is it always onerous. Some folks are naturally engaging, to a point. Others have something an audience wants to hear and a fixed way of doling it out; early rap artists fit that category. Tribal storytellers entrance their listeners. Television meteorologists keep us up another fifteen minutes each night because their body language signals excitement while we feed on the substance of weather news. When people are predisposed to receiving messages, hungry for them, a little expressiveness can go a long way.

On the other hand, a natural ebullience can inflate the message. Visitors to Ireland are charmed by natives who can engage them in matters of dubious substance. My own experiences are typical. Once, after asking directions of a hard-as-nails farmer near Kenmare, I sat transfixed for the next hour as I learned that: A fox travels in one path only and strikes when a cloud hits the moon. Holly bushes regulate the outdoor temperatures. Irish food makes the blood thick. Salmon lose weight as they climb upstream. The Irish pay no property tax. Well water beats ginger ale. Hawaii stinks—all of this in a Gaelic lilt to help push expression into expressiveness.

Rural Americans may be less expressive, but media attention can draw them out. In the rural Mississippi Valley, victims of the 1993 floods found words for some of their anguish:

> . . . You can't believe the smell. My husband, who cleans
> hog pens six days a week, can take a lot. He walked into the
> house and almost vomited. You go through the process of
> being mad and you work through it. You have your cry and
> then you clean it out. But I told [my] husband, I don't

think I can do it again. I feel like going out and kicking the
pigs.[5]

Such expressiveness simply isn't available to many of us. Our
lives lack drama and local color. Our messages are of low news
value. Our cultural heritage charms few. Our rap skills are
wanting. Rarely are audiences predisposed to our utterances.
On the contrary, modern audiences are benumbed by daily
overdoses of media and message. Just try to engage them in
the midst of their lives, in competition with every other stimulus imaginable. It challenges even those raised in the storytelling tradition or in high-pitched and demonstrative cultures.

In pursuit of expressiveness, what we are left with is the work
of pressing out words. The work is mulish, even when nonverbal expression kicks in to help speakers. Expressiveness may
feel unnatural, like a rupture in the instinct that made us
stealthy hunters. Even now silence helps keep predators at bay.
Hard work, this pressing out of words into other brains, and
probably unnatural. For that matter, what is natural about
brains yielding to someone else's extrusions? No wonder we
need prodding to sustain the effort. We are climbing a moun-
tain here, but the heights are attainable. The trail lies just
ahead.

5

Steps Toward Expressiveness

*A*nyone who has seen *Pygmalion* or *My Fair Lady* knows how quickly expressiveness can flower when love and a wager come into play: On a bet, Professor Henry Higgins tutors a Cockney loudmouth named Eliza Doolittle in Snob Speech 101, and Eliza achieves enough courtly elegance to pass muster at a ball. If we ask no more than that of expressiveness, then the Higgins Method will suffice.

Of course we do ask more, if we hope to engage distracted listeners and readers. And while small steps toward expressiveness yield quick rewards, the quick fix for mushy-mouthed language doesn't exist. (Probably just as well: What would we do with three billion instant orators?) Instead the fix involves a number of long-term commitments worth keeping in mind:

> *Read—Listen—Savor—Keep a Journal.*
> *Pause—Scan—Choose—Invent—Polish.*

These are the acts to which expressive people must commit themselves. And if the word *commit* smacks of twelve-step recovery, think of these acts as *acquired habits of highly expressive people.*

Wordsmiths who engage and stimulate diverse audiences are usually people who:

Read. They heed the call of expressive writing, wherever it takes them: new literature, classics, drama, poetry, journalism, sacred text, subcultural outcries, lively trash. The sea of language must osmose into the brain. Readers simply soak up more than nonreaders because (1) vast numbers of words pass before the reader's view; (2) readings are more varied than everyday speech; (3) the reader can pause to absorb expressive language; and (4) unlike the hurried spoken word, the written word is crafted to engage the reader.

For example, the casual speaker may dub New York "a terrific town, a super place with neat people," which hardly distinguishes it from Grand Rapids. But a crafted commentary, a piece of reading, describes the city's

> high, windy, incandescent days, [its] magic and majesty as epicenter of the nation and the world, . . . its glamorous parties and beautiful women and dialogue sparkling with adroit repartee, its . . . full-blooded lunacies, its teeming adventure and perilous fun, its monumental ambition, its aura . . . of idealism and titillation and tempestuous feasibility. . . .[1]

Listen. Expressive people listen not just for content, but for how words are used, for the parts that make up the whole. They *pay attention* to language. They listen for what works and what doesn't in speeches, conversation, mass communications. When stimulated by language—by an unexpected word, a powerful figure of speech—they take notice. When bored they observe some of the patterns causing the ennui.

Savor. When a delicious piece of expression comes their way, whether by written or spoken word, expressive people do not simply wolf it down. They chew on it to savor its essence, and thus make it theirs. *Savor* itself, for example, is a word whose juicy sibilance invites mastication. "Savory spices." "A story you'll savor." Mm-*mm*.

Keep a Journal. One means of savoring is to preserve the most delicious tidbits encountered in reading and listening. Expressive people preserve them in a journal, which they review from time to time. A journal of expressiveness takes special note of language, the telling words and phrases, the rousing images, the particular odds and ends that will flavor one's own expression or simply tickle the tongue at a later time. Some varied fragments from my own journal:

> fat-bottomed swamp cypress . . . compassion fatigue . . . impact-absorbing crumple zones . . . cross-fecundation . . . etiolated flesh . . . rhetoric à la disco . . . Angelo "The Nutcracker" LaPietra . . . top-grade barbarian . . . diluvian . . . hectored . . . doinked . . . slathered . . . swell and swale . . . warp and weft . . . the retreating and advancing shush of the surf, *poosh, shoosh.*

Journals can quickly inflate to bursting with the *bon mots* of one deft writer, such as John Updike (last item, above). Expressive people thus develop the related habit of marking up their personal libraries for later reference and inspiration.

Some journal-keepers also collect hated words and phrases, sometimes as a way of purging them. "Wow, that's a panorama and a half!" or "Whatever floats your boat" would be typical inclusions.

When in the Act

Read, listen, savor, keep a journal—these are ongoing habits of expressive people. The next five apply during acts of expression.

Pause. Expressive speakers develop the habit of pause as a means of communication. Limited to a few seconds, the pause does three wonderful things, sometimes at the same time: It gives weight to what precedes it, builds drama for what follows, and allows for sharpening the next words if they have not been predetermined.

The silent pause is a simple device; anyone can stop vocalizing for a moment—but nonprofessional speakers tend to motor on like outboards. Why? Because a second's pause seems to hang forever. The speakers fear they will lose their audience. They fear that listeners will think they've gone blank, that attention will fly out the air vents. In conversation they fear that someone will interrupt them, as when relatives are jockeying for the last word. (In such cases no one is listening, anyway.)

During formal presentations, a long pointless halt panics everyone. But an artful pause grips an audience rather than loses it. The artfulness might entail nonverbal "turn-maintaining" cues, such as raising the brows or a finger as if to say, "Stand by for the extraordinary!" The speaker must seem in control of the pause, holding the audience still. Exaggerated eye contact with a front-row listener helps. If the control is there, the longer the pause, the more effective, up to about four seconds. The artful pauser also chooses a key stopping point:

> "I want to thank my host for a lovely"—abrupt three-second pause, causing some tension—"no, lovely seems inadequate. Thank you for this"—two-second pause, allowing for anticipation of a good word—*"celestial* evening." [Relief. Delight.]

Recently, while addressing a group of librarians who had praised his early work, a Pulitzer Prize–winning novelist said, "Thank you for your"—long pause—*"prescience."* The audience hung on the pause, as listeners tend to do when awaiting information about themselves. They applauded the carefully chosen word. When the novelist read from one of his dark war tales, however, some of the pauses were annoying. Like any dramatic device, pauses can be (1) excessive in number and (2) theatrical or labored. Please be *moved,* they seemed to beg in this case. Expressive speakers pause often, but not always for dramatic effect. To distinguish a thought they pause to find a more *precise* word than the first one that pops up. This is the same creative process as in writing, except that the pause must be brief because listeners are waiting. Like good writers, however, these speakers

scan choices of possible words
choose apt ones for the situation
invent fresh ways to use or combine them, and
polish the syntax (word order) for emphasis and flow

In scanning for descriptive language, the first terms we slam into are those generic adjectives spread across the landscape like shopping malls. "Great" or "fine" or "nice" or "awful" and so on. We next encounter the cliché groupings, words that stick together like pieces of chewed gum such as "sweet as pie," "crystal clear," and "soaking wet." One makes a quick judgment based on the situation. The generic or gummy choice may be appropriate. How's the family? "Fine." How's the new car? "Good as gold." How was the weather? "Rained like cats and dogs." This is all the expressiveness expected in elevators and other mundane situations. But when listeners demand stimulation—critical thinking, wit, art, entertainment—the first stock words that come to mind won't do. A pause sets the stage for choice and design.

"You spent Christmas with the family? How was it?"
"Let me think . . ." *"Fine"? Not true. "Awful"? Too broad. "Dysfunctional"? Accurate but overused. Needs help. "Dysfunctionally festive. Dysfunctional festivity." Right tone, but cryptic.*

"It was more or less normal—dysfunctional cheer and group depression."

The mental process may seem laborious as written out, but when habitual it takes place quickly, especially if long-term habits such as reading have fattened the stock of ready words and patterns. The immediate goal is not to create literature, only to leapfrog predictable patterns. Creators of written literature have time to agonize over words *and* revise whole passages at their own pace. Some speakers feel free to revise orally, but they sound like this:

"I am so tired. Make that 'totally wiped.' No, let's say 'utterly fatigued.' Or better, 'Ah'm as tard as the Lord God on the seventh day of Creation.' No, wait—"

Pause also serves as transition between twists of thought. It allows listeners a brief rest and recharge. Professional storytellers know this well, keeping the squirmiest children on edge with frequent pauses. Where pause is taboo, as in postgame sports interviews or nightly newscasts, speakers resort to ridiculous transitions:

". . . and the father remains in critical condition at County Hospital. On the flip side, it was turkey time at the Veterans Home in West Portage. . . ."

Often, rather than pause, we stuff verbal straw into the spaces between our spoken statements. We plug the opportunity for silent expressiveness with all those "you know's" and "like's" and "see what I'm sayin's." At the same time we block our escape from the banal, fearing the risks of choice: For what will guide these choices? What are the rules? What if we choose wrong, make fools of ourselves, appear to be something we are not?

The most expressive people share these worries, just as seasoned performers suffer stage fright. Writers worry about the permanence of stupid choices in print. And yet the world's verbal risk-takers press on. After all, not every flight from the commonplace is a suicide mission. Many of our common patterns are like iron muzzles. Simply to cast them off is liberating, allowing freer language to make its way out. Below (and in later chapters) are some of these patterns, with keys to escaping.

New Patterns for Old

On the left are patterns of stifled expression. The PSCIP process (pause/scan/choose/invent/polish) offers one way to unstifle them. At right are alternatives that might result, more expressive if not always perfect; comments follow. Notice that exotic vocabulary is rarely necessary.

Common	Better
. . . her wrinkled face crinkling into a grin as I entered.	". . . the old face benignly wreathing into welcome . . ." (Ian McEwan, *Black Dogs*, Doubleday, 1992)

Tired imagery. Too many faces have crinkled, too many eyes twinkled, too many crow's feet have deepened for anyone to be stirred anew. McEwan's inventive use of "wreathing" breaks the predictable pattern. Further polishing might have deleted "benignly," since "wreathing into welcome" is clearly not malignant. The next time you describe something, try an unexpected image for fit.

We are reconsidering our structural configurations and reposi-	We enter the new day informed by the past. We are focused.

tioning ourselves in both the public and private sectors; we are ready to find the ways in which to reverse our unsuccessful strategies and take advantage of the opportunities that the social, political, and economic environment promises to afford.

Agile. Alert. Never again will opportunity pass us by.

Verbal overload, value underload. Everyone knows the perils of verbosity, but when the stakes are high, as in stockholder reports or state addresses, pumped-up rhetoric may be expected. If so, at least break the patterns of (1) saying what is obvious and (2) padding with nonexpressive strings such as "the ways in which." Choose words that deliver value. At his 1933 inaugural during the Great Depression, Franklin D. Roosevelt pumped up the verbiage when he said, "So first of all let me assert my firm belief that the only thing we have to fear is fear itself—nameless, unreasoning, unjustified terror which paralyzes needed efforts to convert retreat into advance." Verbose, but high in words of symbolic value. If you can't deliver value, ease the load.

The waves were incredibly huge, I mean, not to be believed. And dark? Beyond belief. You would not believe how dark. Unbelievably scary, believe me.

"I see the height of the heavy seas like gigantic black throats in the dim cast of our cabin light. . . ." (E. L. Doctorow, *Billy Bathgate*, Random House, 1989)

Unbelievable incredulity. "Everyone is in a state of unbelievability," said a 1994 Olympic official in reference to rebel skater Tonya Harding. We are indeed in that state. Terms of incredulity dominate our descriptions of extraordinary experience. Odd, when you think about it, because in truth we are stimulated by what we believe rather than disbelieve. One *can* believe that waves looked like black throats, and that is scary. Unbelievability provides no image, nothing to respond to but the limitations of the speaker's beliefs. When precise description is important, try to avoid the mall of incredulity and see where your thoughts lead.

I'm sort of like not a whole lot into the growing-up-type thing right now?	I reject and revile maturity.
Many Americans are often less than satisfied with what might be considered organized labor interests.	Americans are sick of unions.

Hedging. Evasive language, or hedging, has its place: Scholars avoid unfounded statements; diplomats hedge to avoid deadly consequences; kids need to sound like kids. But such legitimate uses leach into everyday adult expression. Hedging should not be confused with effective understatement, such as "We are not amused" to mean "We are livid." Hedging (also known as pussyfooting or watering down) avoids choice and risk. It makes half a statement for fear of risking precise language or bold generalizations. It is characterized by such elements as:

Qualifiers such as "most," "often," "many," and "some." If I write "Americans love baseball" in an editorial, readers appreciate what is meant from the context. They don't need the tedious "Many Americans, perhaps most, often love baseball."

Unsaying. To avoid straightforward statements such as "You're fired," we *un*say the opposite of the direct. "It is less than pleasing to inform you that your performance does not compare favorably with the minimum standards, and that your continued employment would not be unfairly described as untenable."

Passive voice. We make poor use of the passive voice (a grammatical subject is acted upon instead of acting) by hiding behind it and the verbiage it encourages. For example, "It was decided that a failing mark would be given to the student," instead of "I failed the student." Find a subject and make it act; make it take responsibility for the act. The passive voice, however, is well used when distinguishing the receiver of action: "Victims are rewarded in my courtroom; punks are jailed."

Interrogative or Valley Girl voice. The young Valley Girls of California set the standard for "uptalking": a question mark or interrogative rise at the end of every spoken clause. "I had to go to Brentwood? So I took Mom's car? I'm driving the freeway? And this guy pulls up?" Uptalking now pervades American speech. Few can resist the pattern, because it is animated and begs response from audiences who are falling asleep. "I had to go to Brentwood?" "Bummer!" ". . . this guy pulls up?" "You are kidding me!" But even as it begs attention, the question mark undermines every statement. Truth, sincerity, and confidence come into question. Job candidates tell interviewers, "I edited the college yearbook? I learned page-making software? I worked for a trade magazine in Pittsburgh? I really want this job?" The interviewer soon wonders, Are they telling or asking?

Excessive political correctness. No one wants to bring back language like this: "Every citizen deserves his rights. We don't need Indian givers in office. Work like a coolie and take your lumps like a man." Humane people shun insensitive language, even if it upends familiar phrasing. A period of zealous language policing, however, has led to blind caution. Rather than chance the currency of a precise term, such as "black people," we hedge to the broader "people of color" or "people of non-

European ethnic heritage." Eventually we resist naming any group without a string of hedging words.

I don't want to rain on your parade, but I was thinking this morning—and I always get my best thoughts in the shower—that the thing we really have to remember, and that there are just so many ways to forget because our possessions—which are completely empty and absolutely worthless in terms of spiritual value—keep growing while our leaders keep telling us to grow the economy, grow the company, grow the product, is to grow ourselves.

The magic of spiritual growth struck me this morning, even as my head rang with talk of growing the economy, growing the company, growing the product. Grow yourself! What could be more obvious, yet easier to forget in our materialistic frenzy?

Top-heavy sentences. Get the actor (subject) to the action (verb) without delay. What could be kinder to listeners? Until they know the action, they can't judge the relevance of all that goes before; yet they must keep the whole top-heavy mess in mind in case it matters. Observe today's patterns: the long, complex clauses that form a subject, the endless dependent clauses, parenthetical asides, and finally a verb barely capable of sustaining the load. Speakers seem determined to test captive audiences by withholding the action. Sentences grow fat and susceptible to other common maladies, as shown in the example: clichés, crutch words ("really," "just"), and redundancies ("completely empty").

Not My Pattern

What if certain patterns in the left column reflect the way you speak? What if those on the right are not "you"? Should you leap from a bridge? I suggest you hold off, just as I have. Much of my daily expression would fall on the left side, and what of it? *Every* word is a gift, part of the miracle of language itself. If I could not enjoy that gift without an endless need for expressiveness, *then* I might seek a tall bridge and a deep river. I enjoy feeling the plain gush of words and distrust people who never use a common pattern.

I do need to cross to the right-hand columns, however, when I feel imprisoned by the left. When the common patterns are *blocking* an expression that will take me somewhere I haven't been. An expression that will reach someone I am not reaching. That will unload something important not getting out. That will tell me—and others—who I am.

6

Expressing "the Real You"

A few tips can loosen the tongue, but a way with words comes slowly. Something has to drive the effort. One motivator is the power of self-expression, or the ability to reveal the inner you. This bursting open like a milkweed, this dehiscence, is an exhilarating prospect; but self-revelation is also self-exposure, which can feel as strange as wearing underclothes on the outside. Contradictory humans that we are, we want the world to know our authentic selves without encroaching on private territory.

Yet what private domain are we protecting? Do we *know* who we are until we come to articulate that inner ooze called self? Of all the rewards of expressiveness, self-knowledge gained through language may be the most thrilling.

The Real Self

Who are we?

At first we are whom the world says we are: "What a good girl!" or "You're just like your *meshuge* father!" We may chatter away, snap up new words, say the darnedest things—but as children we are essentially a patchwork of received and imitated selves.

Into our teen years we glimpse an "authentic" self, one that cries out for expression. In actions we might pursue some mad-cap rebellion, dying the hair green or swallowing goldfish, but in words—even in soul-searching poetry—we find it safest to go with the herd or the sub-herd as the forces of peer-approval reign us in. The outer reaches of language seem lonely and foreboding. Which words, which idiom, which voice would represent us as we "really" are—and which would project some alien geek?

The longing for self-revelation remains, but now the way of words is clogged. Something has atrophied since childhood. Fears and inhibitions pile up. Recently professor and poet Marvin Bell looked in on a university's core literature classes. He noted that students "from 'ordinary' backgrounds like mine . . . lack the courage to be articulate, so they speak in an all-purpose colloquial flow designed to show how well they fit in rather than how they stand out: plenty of 'you know's' and 'I mean's' and 'kind of's,' lots of 'like's.' . . . They seem to understand what they mean, but they never quite say it. Ultimately, . . . when the conversation grows more complex, they will be able to say neither what they understand nor what they do not understand."[1]

The Articulate Self

"They lack the courage to be *articulate,*" says Bell. Now, there's a word people like to throw around. *An articulate young woman. An articulate candidate. An articulate applicant.* Or the back-handed compliment, *She's surprisingly articulate for a* _____ (fill in the blank).

Articulation has been used in English for at least seven hundred years. Along with the later-appearing *articulate,* it probably derives from *árthron* and *artus,* the Greek and Latin words respectively for "joint." The Romans used the verb *articulare* in the sense of dividing meat (and perhaps captives) into single joints. Today the words have to do with connecting joints or parts or differentiating single parts from the connected ones. In speech, articulate means "to utter clearly in distinct syllables." Joint by joint, we distinguish connected sounds. We enunciate. (Comedy host Milton Berle used to pinch the lips of his guests, urging them to "e-nun-ci-ate!" He might have said "ar-tic-u-late" had he considered it as funny a word.)

The sense of articulate as "clear and intelligible expression" goes back at least to 1830, and today the meanings extend to "precise and effective use of words" and "easy and fluent use of language." In these uses we still see a relationship to joints, their singularity and connectivity. When communication is so inarticulate as to be unintelligible, we call it "disjointed."

Here is our articulate job applicant, facing the dreadful task of describing her "management style":

> I'd call it upbeat. Open. Assertive. I'm drawn to ambitious projects, even the insanely ambitious, but I approach each in sane increments, and my record shows the results. Having achieved equilibrium in my own life, I can focus on people and problem-solving at work. Colleagues praise my rapport with staff of all backgrounds.

Nothing lyrical here, but the message is delivered in sturdy, connected statements. Compare with the loose-jointed version:

> Hey, I'm a manager and a half. I'm a positive-type kind of person, I mean, my head's in the right place and I can handle a whole lot of grief sans getting weirded out. Where are we going with this? Okay. I've got my act together, so I'm majorly into people. No matter who it is, I'm like, how's it going? You know?

Or the stiff-jointed:

> I'm a goal-oriented self-starter whose facilitative skills assure the effectiveness and efficiency of the team-building

process and the promulgation of strategic managerial objectives.

Early in our lives it seems easy to join words to convey a personal truth. With a few articulated phrases we differentiate our child selves and situations from the rest of the universe. Within a few years, however, everyone seems to be saying the same things in much the same patterns: "I am totally against violence to women." "I'm an animal-rights type person." "I'm really into parenting." No longer distinctive, our statements have become mass-manufactured labels. To differentiate our-selves we must now (1) break free of such categorical or ge-neric utterances; (2) join words in fresh, elastic ways. This, says Professor Bell, takes courage. Bell faults students who lack "the courage to be articulate." Why is courage necessary? Because most of us live in the domain of the inarticulate, where clear, honest, and precise expression sticks out like exposed but-tocks. How many kids are whacked for being "wise-assed"? Who dares to be the well-spoken "snobs," "suck-ups," and "phonies" of public school? What happens to the articulate in the world's killing fields?

Articulate self-expression risks the scorn not only of peers and goons, but of the more articulate: the word masters and other intellectual superiors standing by in judgment. The risks are enough to seal one's lips until curmudgeonhood, and even then there is no free passage. Nobel Prize winner Saul Bellow, describing himself as an "elderly white male," noted recently: "We can't open our mouths without being denounced as rac-ists, misogynists, supremacists, imperialists, or fascists."[2]

Statements

Still, people want to reveal themselves, and many try doing so in shows of identity called "statements." You are AGRESV 1, your vanity auto plate. You are the recordings you buy and lip-synch. You are what you eat, what you drive, what you wear. What you tattoo on your skin or dab behind your ears—you *Poison* you. Naturally, advertisers recognize this quest and cast their wares as self-expression. To promote a clothing boutique, a Chicago billboard campaign showed a sexily attired and supine woman with the legend "Your most influential statements are made on your back."

In the popular view everything "makes a statement," a quality that lends dignity to looting a minimart or trashing the Champs-Élysées. Action-based statements get special attention if not always desired or enduring responses. From Gary Cooper to Clint Eastwood, the hero of big actions and few words is an American icon. Eastwood's advice in one macho military film is to "Shut that hole under your nose!" Unfortunately, in doing so the inarticulate must then state themselves within the limitations of No Fear T-shirts, big hair, generic grunts, and a few slick moves. Many young people believe they can make their statements through music, particularly soulful rock. "I don't talk or express myself that well, that's why I do music," said singer Kurt Cobain. But Cobain shotgunned his brains out in the spring of 1994.[3]

Life, most will agree, can dump heaps of toxic waste upon the struggling self. Articulate self-expression helps us dig out. Music, generic babble, and action statements may relieve some pressure but rarely get us out from under. When novelist Henry Roth said "language transmutes [transforms] the dross [refuse] of experience," he was talking not only about elevating the commonplace into art but of expression as survival. He was eighty-eight when he said it, still writing and articulating himself.[4]

The Real Voice

"Language transmutes the dross of experience." Can those fancy-schmancy words be the real voice of Henry Roth, a child of the New York slums? If "real" means the voice that best delivers a thought, the answer is yes. Do the words deliver the authentic Henry Roth? Partly. They reveal a part of the mix that makes up Roth's unique self. *Transmute* and *dross* are literary words that Roth used to express a certain sentiment to a literary audience. He would not use them hollering for the garbage to be taken out. He would use other voices for other purposes, a range with no upper or lower limits.

Compared to the average person, writers take easily to self-transformation through language. In fact, if their publishers encourage it, some writers shed voices like old skins and leap into more crowd-pleasing selves. But for most other people—especially youth—a sudden leap into expressiveness may seem like dancing across the bowling alley in a tutu. True, your inner transformations may be crying for expression, but you express one thing and (inarticulate) people suspect you of another. Originality is suspect. Soon the transformations themselves become suspect and you sweep them under the rug.

From English class or an overheard remark, a new word comes to light on your tongue and feels good there. "Transcendent." You try it privately; it carries a meaning you used to grope for with phrases such as "far out"—but no one ever realized just how far out you meant. "How'd you feel when the ball landed in your mitt?" Or "What was it like when he put that flower in your hair?" Transcendent! A transcendent moment! That's exactly what it was; but unfortunately you can never tell anyone because *that word ain't you.*

But it is you. It is you, the evolving you. Maybe "transcendent" doesn't fit the you defined by the rest of the world, but it can fit the emerging self or the self you decide to nurture and extrude. Monkeying with the self may seem artificial and even schizoid, but to accept false limitations betrays human potential. The notion of a predetermined self buried in you like some time-release capsule is Broadway fantasy, from the school of *someday I'll find my destiny.* Writer V. S. Naipaul remarks, "One isn't born one's self. One is born with a mass of expectations, a mass of other people's ideas—and you have to work through it all."[5]

If expressiveness doesn't seem to fit the natural you, then consider reshaping the bona fide real you. Don't waste time finding your single real voice. We rarely *find* our real voice, plumbing the depths until we snare one that sounds right. Our voice can be a new voice—or several—that we *make* real, a voice in harmony with our roots but capable of expressing the full flower of the evolving self. Like everything that breaks from the ordinary, the new voice entails risks, apprehensions, missteps. These are reasonable costs of liberation.

Cute Flavio

"Flavio is like so cute," is one way to describe a new heartthrob, an ordinary way that takes no chances. Here's another:

> God made you from red clay, Flavio, with his hands. This face of yours like the little clay heads they unearth in Teotihuacán. Pinched this cheekbone, then that. Used obsidian flints for the eyes, those eyes dark as the sacrificial wells they cast virgins into. . . . Flavio, with skin sweet as burntmilk candy, smooth as river water.[6]

Now we know precisely how cute Flavio is, distinguished from every other cutie. This is a voice of writer Sandra Cisneros, expressed through a character in *Woman Hollering Creek*, a voice Cisneros forges from her Mexican-American heritage and Chicago-neighborhood street talk, her readings and studies and listening, and the courage and will to go beyond ordinary self-expression.

Cisneros speaks in many voices, child-innocent, goddess-all-knowing, drawing on any word that expresses the heart, including Spanish words—*mi vida, mi preciosa, mi chiquita, mi chulito, mi bebito*—Strunk and White's advice against foreign phrases notwithstanding. (*"That* language," she writes of Mexican Spanish. "That sweep of palm leaves and fringed shawls. That startled fluttering, like the heart of a goldfinch or a fan. . . ." *¡Ay, que linda!*)

Speaking in many voices—a trait that might have gotten one burned at the stake in earlier times—is a sweet privilege of modern Western culture and one that offers new freedom in expressing the multifaceted self. According to at least one reputable psychiatrist, the self that is capable of shifting and adapting to different roles is a source of strength and not pathologically fragmented. Unlike the "fundamentalist self" or consistency freak who sees change as menace, the "willful eclectic" better reflects (and expresses) the disorderliness of life and varieties of reality.[7]

Many of us have marveled at our multiple personalities as we shift from street to bedroom to boardroom selves, from mystic to manic to skeptic. Although we might still cling to the idea of one authentic self and one real voice, in truth we are free to embrace as "real" any voice that helps us process experience and adapt to the world.

"Get Out of Here with This Nerd Stuff"

A case in point is the question of so-called black dialect or black English versus Standard ("white") English, and how to reconcile the two in school and beyond. Reporting on the conflict, *New York Times* writer Felicia R. Lee notes that black vernacular has steadily diverged from Standard English, and that as an inner-city dialect it may have a stronger grip than ever on young people.[8] To encourage students to learn Standard English, Lee reports, some educators teach it as a second language; others stress the payoffs of speaking the Standard English of business and the professions. But several teachers face cynicism and even rage over what the black students call "talking proper." At one school students shout, "Who are you trying to be?" when peers use Standard English in class. Elsewhere, a senior describes a similar attitude: "That's like, 'Get out of here with this nerd stuff.' They say you're trying to be white. It's a stereotype that white people are so proper and that black people are real."

One New York City teacher notes that attitudinal changes are difficult but essential. For career success, for broader empowerment, "the African American inner-city kid has to turn it off and turn it on and be, in effect, bilingual." Linguist Geneva Smitherman, interviewed by Lee, feels that this bilingualism must work both ways. In the sixties to the eighties, she said, black English was a language to be recognized for its patterns, its system, its rules. "Now we are at the point where we need a multilingual policy that means that everybody would learn one other language or one other dialect."

Is it phony to equip oneself with all the means of expression within reach? One needn't abandon roots, home, and soul to exploit the breadth and structure of Standard English. What if "talking proper" helps give voice to your feelings, distinguish your ideas, signal affinities with like-minded people, and empower you in the broader world? What "self" does that betray?

Is it phony for Standard-English speakers to embrace ethnic vernacular? They try it often enough, if not always successfully. Is there a white person who hasn't wished to borrow the expressiveness of black English or other ethnic patterns? Comedian George Carlin gets a knowing laugh when he reminisces about white boys talking "black" on the street corners—and never a black group chattering "white." How quickly do white vacationers adopt black-islander dialects, saying to each other over dinner, "How you keepin', mon?" and "What you got for me, cool mamma?"

You will always face interference when extending your "real" voice. "Who are you trying to be?" people will demand. Let them think what they want. You are trying to be someone you were not: an expressive person adapting to a changing world.

The Stable Self

As multifaceted as the self might be, it cannot keep dividing like cells out of control. Eventually the sum of your parts will take on a personality. If your courage holds out, it will be an adaptable and ever-evolving personality, but it will have a dominant tone that shapes your self-expression. You will have many real and expressive voices: public, private; casual, formal; spoken, written. But among them you will seek harmony, rather than shift personalities willy-nilly. Together, they will articulate who you are: a force to be reckoned with.

7

Elements of Force

May your head grow upside down in the dirt, like a beet!
Albert Einstein he's not.

From oath to understatement, force comes to expression in a thousand potent forms, yet our discourse runs to the feeble. Increasingly we live among stock situations that call for nothing more than stock phrases or ways of saying, "Don't worry, I'm only here to exchange sound waves." But when the moment arrives to express the extraordinary, to achieve self-expression, to pierce resistant minds—to "thrust home!" as Cyrano de Bergerac would put it—we must deploy the elements of force.

Always force is relative to audience sensibilities. How to express the force of love, for example? It depends on the audience. A contemporary film[1] chooses special visual effects—tongue, heart, and eyeballs boinging out toward the loved one—and every last moviegoer gets the message. Just as powerful to a literary audience are the single-syllable words of Elizabeth Barrett Browning: "I love thee to the depth and breadth and height my soul can reach."[2] Between lovers, a private intimacy—"mooshkie," "pooshkie," whatever—might have the force of Hurricane Hazel.

Expressive force derives from words themselves, their symbolism and freshness to the audience. From their sound. From

63

the way words are used in figures of speech. From their arrangement. From what is not said. From a buildup of meaning. From nonverbal cues. From new sources one discovers every day. "Human communication," notes linguist Steven Pinker, "is not just a transfer of information like two fax machines connected with a wire; it is a series of alternating displays of behavior by sensitive, scheming, second-guessing, social animals. When we put words into people's ears we are impinging on them. . . ."[3]

That impingement brings to mind the narrator of *The Rime of the Ancient Mariner,* who seizes listeners with a "skinny hand" to capture their attention. The physical approach has many variations. Recently in a Portuguese village, a pensioner spotted me as an American on whom he could practice his English. His vocabulary had faded, but he achieved force by stabbing my shoulder with two stiff fingers. Immobilized as if by a snakebite, I listened:

> Ah, you are American, my friend. *[stab!]* Thirteen years I work in New Jersey. *[stab!]* After, I go to San Francisco. *[stab!]* I show off all my money, smoke big cigar like millionaire. *[stab!]* . . . Mr. Bill Clinton not you president. *[stab!]* The spouse of Mr. Bill Clinton you president. *[stab!]* . . .

The supposedly reserved Portuguese demonstrate a surprising range of force in expression. One particular gesture—in response to excessive gratitude—looks like a mime slinging a make-believe cow over a wall. ("Don't mention it" is the poor English equivalent.) Portugal also is home to that melancholy form of cabaret singing called *fado,* which draws its force from intense body language, surging volume, and crash of vowel against consonant. In one typical move, singer clutches chest as if to crack the sternum, then, voice exploding, rushes the listener with palms held outward. "Now do you feel my troubles?" is the message.

Spoken and written English provide their own powerful devices. Even without body language we can impinge upon our audiences. Most of us have a sense of forceful expression, including its underlying principles à la freshman composition:

- Use powerful verbs, closely linked to subject and object.
- Use concrete language that stimulates the senses.
- Trim the fat; omit redundant words and needless clauses.

And so on. In speaking, however, we rarely pause to think about rules or technique. In writing we have been hung up on correctness or business jargon or literary chic, everything but achieving force. The result: general despair when called upon to sell an idea or to express the extraordinary in terms more powerful than "major major big time."

Powerful Charms

"I have heard of certain words that have all the force in them of the most powerful charms," said Socrates.[4]

And what is the most powerful charm a word can possess? We need not be Socrates to dope that one out. It is *association*. When an audience associates a word with strongly felt experience, that word strikes to the quick. Which class of word stirs the mightiest associations? The class called particulars—names of *specific* things that can be pictured or felt.

For example, the generalized terms *edibles* or *comestibles* barely stir my consciousness. But mention "double-rich black cherry ice cream with chewy fudge and crunchy almonds," and cholesterol fears be damned, I'm all yours. The word *insignia* has little impact, but *swastika* elicits a feeling. For expressive power, the more specific the association the better. Every guide to expressive language stresses *precision* or *exactitude*. Why? Because while we may learn in generalities, we experience in particulars. Give me a particular that evokes an experience, and the switch goes to *on*. I awake. I respond.

Most powerful are words that recall sensory experience: sight, sound, smell, taste, touch, and inner sensation, including nervous pain and pleasure. Such words—concrete as opposed to abstract—can trigger an image as powerful as the original stimuli. "She raked her nails across the blackboard—*screeeeeek!*" Get the goosebumps? Or feel the heat of James Joyce's Hell: ". . . the brains are boiling in the skull, the heart in the breast glowing and bursting, the bowels a redhot mass of burning pulp, the tender eyes flaming like molten balls."[5]

Associations don't have to irritate to be forceful. They have only to strike a chord, as they say, to resonate and thus overcome resistance. "The bells rang loudly" is a generic image; it doesn't symbolize anything in particular, doesn't stir a specific association. But novelist Heinrich Böll does so with these precise details:

> . . . the cathedral bells started pealing, their ringing made the windowpanes oscillate, vibrate, and this vibration was picked up by a metal curtainrod lying on the windowsill, its dance producing a subdued chittering.[6]

Keen are the joys of word-hunting, that foraging for words that glow, bleed, pulse, and kick. Unfortunately, such dry abstractions as "precision," "concretion," and "particularity" obscure the pleasures of the quest. Juicier terms are hard to come by. Some writers use "texture" to describe qualities that lift words off a page. "Palpable" is another term for language you can touch and feel (though I associate it more with palpation—the diagnostic squooshing of one's head and other parts). What about "muscularity"? "She shouldered her way through the gawkers" is rich in muscularity, but so is "lacy feathers of window frost,'' which evokes four images (mental pictures) in five words. Language needn't be macho to be forceful, even if tough talk has muscled its way into all aspects of our culture.

Below, loosely named, are various elements to draw upon in driving our thoughts home.

Power Boosters

High-Energy Verbs. Verbs power sentences. Energetic verbs rocket them. In expressing the nature of things, we can tell what they *are,* what qualities they *have*—or we can show what they *do* and do *to* something. The doing is usually more forceful, and it is done with action verbs.

Notice at what point this little sequence springs to life: ''She was hungry. She knew of a place nearby. She had money. Soon she was served. She attacked the meat loaf, bloodied it with catsup, wolfed it down.'' The verbs ''attacked,'' ''bloodied,'' and ''wolfed'' introduce dynamic energy, partly through their associations with action—fierce action. Action verbs produce force, especially action verbs that can be sensed. As used here, the action verbs are also ''transitive'' verbs, because they act *upon* something—the poor meat loaf—which helps project force.

Think of a sentence's subject as mass. Something has to move it. A physics-like formula can remind us to harness the power of the verb: $E = sv^2$; Energy equals subject times verb squared—or subject animated by a big verb:

> She pulverized the windshield. He howled. ''Don't slobber,'' she told him. Broken glass festooned the bucket seats. He snapped out a handkerchief, swathed a glass fragment in it, thrust it at her. She winced. They hurled insults. Shattered every bond between them. Plunged into frothing silence.

Not all subject-mass moves so unpleasantly. Verbs release positive force as well. Walt Whitman elevates the whole mass of humankind in "Song of Myself" (1855) with such energetic verbs as: souse, swag, unrumple, draggle, rock, dash, graft, chant, surge, dote, scoot, exude, suffuse, whirl, wrench, dab, adorn, dilate, girdle, straddle, jet, buoy, whiz, bag, strew, fling . . . until finally—

> I depart as air, I shake my white locks at the runaway sun,
> I effuse my flesh in eddies, and drift it in lacy jags.

Novelty can add force to verbs. All too soon our most energetic words suffer from wear. At this writing the good verb "tweak," as in "we tweaked the revenues to balance the bottom line," is being tweaked to death. Look for new energy in little-used verbs ("They hectored him without mercy"); revived verbs from earlier times ("Stop pingling your food and eat up"); verbs recruited from other parts of speech ("Don't price-fix me"); verbs in fresh applications ("flavors that blitz the taste buds"); or verbs imported from other English-speaking cultures. When I read the following line from *The London Times*, I had no idea what it meant—but it tickled me:

". . . the church commissioners sussed the cut of his godless jib . . ." (And later I was charmed to learn that *sussed* means *suspected* and "cut of his *jib*" his *manner*. Who'd a sussed?)

Word Grenades. Which has more force? (1) "The students made a total wreck of our apartment like some kind of wild animals that had been locked up in it" or (2) "The students savaged our apartment." I would pick no. 2, because the word "savaged" is understood by most audiences and compresses the meaning of eighteen words in the first sentence. When forceless words can be compressed into one energetic word, consider doing it:

His deep, intense, adoring feelings eventually became incredibly hard to take.	His passions grew insufferable.
. . . something about her that seems greedy and corrupt, like she could be bribed, like she would sell out.	. . . something venal about her.

Given the same meaning, the smaller package of words—the grenade—usually delivers more force than a fusillade of blanks. Often we try to supercharge grade-B words with such modifiers as "extremely," "strongly," "especially," and "extraordinarily," but Standard or vernacular English can usually yield a grade-A word that encompasses the modifier.

excessively ingratiating	*smarmy*
strongly poisonous	*venomous*
loudly irritating	*strident*

Not that shorter is always better or that the compression always sounds right in context, but watch for words that can encompass others. Poetry, that most compressed literary expression, is a good place to find them. Hackers can experiment with dictionary software that provides word-hunting features. Type "shrill AND loud" in one particular program, and the dictionary coughs up "strident." However, "loud AND angry" yields nothing. The associative powers of language software—so literal and generic—have yet to equal those of the world's worst poets.

Sound Bursts. Words can borrow the force of natural sounds by mimicking some of their elements. Whomp. Whap. Clink. Clang. Splash. Screech. Literary students know this effect as *onomatopoeia*. Tennyson's "murmur of innumerable bees" is often used as an example, but for force I prefer Tom Wolfe's depiction of sexual steam in his seventies essay "The Boiler Room and the Computer":

> . . . Such peeling squealing/ biting sticking/ ramming jamming/ gobble licking/ nuzzling guzzling/ . . . Rutboar grunting/Lapping gashing . . .[7]

A related phenomenon is words of kindred meanings that share a distinctive sound. Certain "sn" words such as "snout" derive from an old proto-Germanic pattern, according to word columnist Craig M. Carver.[8] "Snoot, snot, sneeze, snuff, snivel, sniffle, snoop, snub" are not only spoken through the nose, but carry expressive qualities associated with that organ. Bigness words often begin with or emphasize "m," as in mondo, mega, massive, million, magnum, monumental, mighty, mammoth, maximum, and (b-i-i-i-g) momma. The hard "c" or "k" *guttural* sound appears frequently within words of hurt—kill, crush, curse, con, crack, kick—and in obscenities. Softer sounds (the *sibilants* s, z, sh, zh, and *liquids* l, m, n, r) help project certain steamy, wet, or gelatinous images. In choosing words, look for sounds that fit the message.

a huge noise	a monstrous hiss
the ground is good and soaked	the world is mud-luscious . . . puddle-wonderful (e. e. cummings)

Wake-Up Images. Too much unrelieved force becomes white noise. But stretches of functional expression need occasional wake-up words and images. In *Riding the Iron Rooster*, Paul Theroux concludes an expository paragraph on yak herding with this note: "The Chinese . . . yak . . . is a lovely long-haired animal, like a cow on its way to the opera."

Tension. "Divide the living child in two, and give half to the one, and half to the other." Force comes from expression that provokes worry, disturbs, frightens. Notice the distressing language of headlines on an average day, even in the nonsensational *New York Times:* GROWING PERIL—CITY IS TENSE—CRIME SOARS—DEAD IN CONGRESS—URGES MORE FORCE—BRINGS TURMOIL, and so on (September 24, 1994). Heavy-handed tension is everywhere present, from family melodrama—"The most terrible thing just happened to your uncle!"—to advertising—"I'm stopping to go to the bathroom more than ever now. I wonder what's wrong with me?" (Merck for Proscar). Such heavy-handedness should wear thin, but humans seem endlessly attuned to menace and conflict.

In classical aesthetic theory, tension is well handled when it provides *catharsis,* or a purging of such emotions as fear and pity. In seeing these emotions played out, audiences experience relief and even elation. The tension poses no direct threat, but engages an audience in danger and conflict at the gut level.

All tension is not visceral, however. Intellectual, philosophical, or ethical conflicts generate slow-burning distress of their own. In an analysis of Lincoln's Gettysburg Address, Larry McEnerney points to the force unleashed by one word—"but":

> . . . a word that means tension, instability, conflict. He [Lincoln] says, *"But."* And suddenly you have a problem. "But, in a larger sense, we can *not* dedicate—can *not* consecrate—we can *not* hallow—this ground. The brave men, liv-

ing and dead, who struggled here, have consecrated it, far above our poor power to add or detract."[9]

Nowness. As long as they remain fresh, trendy utterances grab attention and make expression seem up-to-the-minute and thus relevant. But fashion is precarious. Writers are often advised to avoid "fad" or "vogue" words or usages likely to putrefy by the time they see print. In today's culture many such terms come from pop music, television comedy, and hacker networks and are quickly exhausted by the aping multitudes. Remember "NOT!" from *Saturday Night Live,* and how forceful it was to negate a statement with that cry? Now it identifies one as an out-of-it nerd. Neologisms (new word formations) and other new twists on language may endure if they fill a need for precision. "Get a life" is more precise than "Find some human interests outside your obsessive preoccupation," and though it has lost its comic edge, it will probably hang on. The sports-based "in the zone," however, was merely a slick-sounding way of saying "hot" or "on a streak," and such terms are quickly generated and exhausted on the playing fields.

The problem is catching up with a language evolving on a million frontiers. Take one part of speech alone—prepositions. Imagine a new English speaker keeping pace with these usages: Get down. Get up on it. Get with the program. Get it on. Off the dude. In your face. Get behind that. Up front. I'm into it. I'm out of here. Up the revolution. I'm about music. She outted.

Music, Rhythm, and Soul. If it swings, lilts, or boogies down, it has force. Used in the right context, touches of ethnic dialect, regionalisms, and musical rhythms have a way of stirring most audiences.

Things aren't going so well.

"Can't kill nothin and won't nothin die." (Geneva Smitherman, *Black Talk*, Houghton Mifflin, 1994)

Come on, have another beer. ". . . he lifted his fist and said, 'I'll give you a bunch of fives, Rose. A bunch of fives if you don't have one.'" (Rosemary Mahoney, *Whoredom in Kimmage*, Houghton Mifflin, 1993)

Forces of Nature. Expression can draw on the energy of natural forces: on the violence of typhoons, twisters, collapsing stars; on the insistence of glacial mass, frost heave, the tides. But beware the maelstrom of clichés.

Desire came upon her like an earthquake, rumbling deep in every fiber, her resistance drowned in tidal waves of passion. . . .

Hold back? Red magma sliding through the crags. Tornadic chaos. Borne on solar winds. Too late, too late . . .

Irreverence. Oscar Wilde: "When the gods wish to punish us they answer our prayers." Germaine Greer: "By the act of marriage you endorse all the ancient and dead values." Woody Allen: "My Lord, My Lord! What hast Thou done, lately?"

In civilized discourse, irreverence is most forceful when it pricks rather than bludgeons. Anyone can achieve the force of shock by insulting or blaspheming another's cherished values. Such shock may stimulate, but it rarely engages. It discourages consideration of one's point of view. It shuts communication down. Sharply pointed irreverence, however, stirs audiences to defense of their values, to engagement and debate.

In the youth culture irreverence is less a device than a way of life, a counterbalance to adult authority. Force in an environment of irreverence demands special inventiveness; otherwise it is simply disrespect, scatological blow-off. We see some of this inventiveness in the nomenclature of popular music groups and their songs. A random sampling: Rough Trade, Sweaty Nipples, Meat Puppets, Puke Grub, Chainsaw Therapy, Bad Examples, Violent Femmes, Waste Kings, Dazzling Killmen, Love Spit Love.

Inventiveness distinguishes even the adult-baiting dementia of Beavis and Butt-head, pride of cable channel MTV. "The main challenge of scripting *Beavis and Butt-head* is to be as dumb as you can possibly be," said one of the show's writers. "You can't assume Beavis and Butt-head know anything. No cognitive leaps."[10]

Sincerity. If for no other reason, expression that conveys sincerity is forceful because it is rare. In generic phrasing practically all convictions have equal value: "These fries are horrible." "These ethnic massacres are horrible." How to signal that you are not simply mouthing words, but expressing a heartfelt value worthy of attention? You don't do it by wagging and dipping the head as you speak, a common trait among Americans attempting sincerity. You don't do it by putting "just" before every verb, as if about to say something so important you'll never say anything else—"I just think we should just stop hating each other and just start learning to, you know, just trust people." You don't do it by resorting to the polemic of victimization, as in "Mandatory heterosexual consumption has sabotaged my independence in opting for celibacy as a direction of personal and political empowerment." And you don't do it by begging for pity, as one learns from this passage in Richard Yates's novel *Young Hearts Crying*:

> "Have you ever noticed," she asked when they were alone again, "how your sympathy for someone's story—anyone's story—tends to evaporate when they get to the part about how long and hard they cried?"[11]

Sincerity requires language that reaches outside the ordinary to signal importance, yet avoids the pitfalls of contrivance, fraudulence, and self-indulgence. It helps to mean what you say, but simple conviction isn't enough. It takes a certain controlled elevation of one's natural voice, language that stands on its toes but doesn't leave the ground.

> . . . Like anybody, I would like to live a long life; longevity has its place. But I'm not concerned about that now. . . . I've seen the promised land. I may not get there with you. But I want you to know tonight that we as a people will get to the promised land. And I'm happy tonight. I'm not worried about anything. I'm not fearing any man. Mine eyes have seen the glory of the coming of the Lord!
> —Martin Luther King, Jr., on the eve of his assassination, April 3, 1968

8

Force, Figures of Speech, and a Little Longinus

No kid would believe it, but the art of forceful expression goes back even further than last night on the streets. Beginning more than two thousand years ago, the Greeks scrutinized the language of debate and of literature. They sought to identify the techniques and devices or "figures" that make expression stylish and forceful. They, and later the Romans, formalized their observations in a heady discipline called rhetoric (which we touched upon in Chapter 3). Rhetoric concerned itself with both artful and "persuasive" prose.

Comparable developments occurred elsewhere in the ancient world, but the achievements of the Greco-Roman cultures were well preserved and widely disseminated. In fact, most of what can be generalized about expression—at least the expression that dominates Western culture—is probably contained in four classical works: two by Aristotle (384–322 B.C.), *Rhetoric* and *Poetics; Institutio oratoria* (ca. A.D. 95) by Quintilian, Roman orator and stylistic theorist; and *On Great Writing (On the Sublime)*, a Greek treatise attributed to roving scholar Cassius Longinus. Known as a "walking encyclopedia," Longinus walked the wrong paths in Roman politics and was executed for treason in A.D. 273.[1]

Of these four classics, *On Great Writing* may offer the most digestible advice to modern prose writers. For one thing, it is brief; only some fifteen thousand words (about fifty printed pages) have survived from a longer work. It is personal and impassioned, unlike classical treatises couched in dialogues and other pedantic forms. Not every passage is applicable today, nor is every principle original with the author—far from it; yet how elegantly each idea comes forth. One can see why Longinus enjoyed cult-level popularity as late as the nineteenth century, although today such treatises as *Writing the Blockbuster Novel* crowd him off the shelves.

On Great Writing sets out to identify "sublime" language— that which expresses greatness of spirit and evokes emotional response. Concerned with force in general and how certain writers apply it, Longinus provides a point of reference as we segue into today's variations on classical forms.

With segues come sound bites, and here are half a dozen from *On Great Writing (On the Sublime)*. True to sound bites, they come naked of context and texture, but still vie for a place in our notebooks.

- There are, we might say, five sources most productive of great writing . . . vigor of mental conception, . . . strong and inspired emotion . . . adequate fashioning of figures of speech, or rhetorical devices, . . . nobility of diction, which in turn includes the choice of words and the use of figurative and artistic language; . . . [and] dignified and distinguished word arrangement.
- The startling and amazing is more powerful than the charming and persuasive . . . to be convinced is usually within our control whereas amazement is the result of an irresistible force beyond the control of any audience.
- . . . those who aim at greatness try to escape the charge of feeble aridity and are somehow led into turgidity, believing it "a noble error to fail in great things."

• . . . false enthusiasm . . . is a display of passion, hollow and untimely, where none is needed. . . . For writers are frequently carried away by artificial emotions of their own making which have no relation to the subject matter. Like drunkards, they are beside themselves, but their audience is not. . . .

• [Forceful] writers have sifted out the most significant details . . . and joined them harmoniously, without inserting between them anything irrelevant, frivolous, or artificial; such additions spoil the total effect just as the imperfect adjustment of massive stones that are fitted together into a wall spoils the whole structure if chinks and fissures are left between them.

• . . . amplification [occurs when] . . . fine, well-rounded passages succeed one another, increasing the effect at every step. . . . Greatness implies distinction, amplification implies quantity; the former can exist in a single thought, the latter always involves length and a certain abundance.

This last principle is especially pertinent today, when every other speaker seeks force by abundance. In observing modern expression, notice how certain attempted amplifications actually diminish force while others build powerful chain reactions. Sports personalities make an event smaller and smaller as they pile up mindless clichés—"Great effort Hundred percent Team victory Can't say enough. . . ." But if driven by powerful thoughts, even short phrases gain momentum as they accumulate:

> You are not part of the community of Israel. You are not part of the national democratic camp which we all belong to in this house, and many of the people despise you. You are not partners in the Zionist enterprise. You are a foreign implant. You are an errant weed. Sensible Judaism spits you out. You placed yourself outside the wall of Jewish law. You are a shame on Zionism and an embarrassment to Judaism.
> —Israeli Prime Minister Yitzhak Rabin, 1994,
> condemning settlers who sanction murder[2]

The Force of Figures

Turning to "adequate fashioning of figures" in great writing, Longinus notes that "a detailed exposition of all the figures . . . would be an endless task." Of course, it would not have been endless—he was speaking figuratively. But the Greeks had identified *hundreds* of such forms, and it would be equally tedious to list them here. Still, it is humbling to look down a list of classical figures—*accismus, adynaton, aenos,* etc.—and realize that the imaginative patterns we admire today at all levels of speech were already forged, stamped, and in the toolbox of every learned speaker before humankind wore long pants.

Note my figurative language. At this point we should nail down the meaning of "figure" or "figurative," especially as applied to force. We shall keep it simple. Figurative is the opposite of literal. Everyone who says "Don't be so literal" seems to understand the meaning of that term—words used in their primary sense and not intended to say or imply anything else. "I want a glass of milk" carries normal meaning, no tricks, no implications. But in "I'd kill for some milk" the speaker is not literally homicidal, merely exaggerating *(hyperbole)* for effect. Just as in "You are milking the point" no udders are squeezed, but a *metaphor* borrows the energy of that act to strengthen the statement. Figurative language stretches the meaning of words. It does so using "figures of speech," or those hundreds of established and named ways of deviating from the literal.

Much of our figurative language consists of "relational" figures, such as similes and metaphors. They cause the listener to relate one thing to another. When that "other" is more stimulating than the literal equivalent, then the figure adds force.

His bat struck the ball and the ball went into the stands.	He took that ball downtown.

Such an act requires an unusual amount of strength.	You gotta have hair on the bottom of your feet to do that.
We are leaving immediately.	We be ghosts.
To make a book seem very truthful, a writer has to know its subject thoroughly.	"For one's book to *sweat* truth, one has to be stuffed to the ears with its subject." (Flaubert)

The association, remember, must be more stimulating than the literal source. The flattest literal statement can pack a wallop, depending on the context. When someone in a dark alley says, "I've got a knife," we don't need figures of speech to make us bolt. Scenes of horror such as terrorist bombings are often described literally because the particulars, the body parts hanging from trees, need no borrowed images to seize our emotions.

Literal expression has the force of *understatement* when used in a sense of holding back. "You are acting in a manner that incurs parental wrath," you tell the incorrigible teen, suppressing the urge to fly into figurative terms. Writers such as Ernest Hemingway and Joan Didion achieve striking effects with restrained prose. Here the narrator of Didion's *A Book of Common Prayer* understates the tragedy of a slain heroine:

> . . . I wanted to lay a flag on the coffin but there were no American flags in Boca Grande and in the end I bought a child's T-shirt in the gift shop at the airport. This T-shirt was printed like an American flag. . . . I think this T-shirt did not have the correct number of stars and stripes but it did have the appearance of stars and stripes and it was red and it was white and it was blue. . . .[3]

The literal voice conveys sincerity with quiet force. "I am grief-stricken by your mother's death and the loss you must feel." Compare that condolence with "The stately ship that bore you to this landing has slipped its moorings to disappear into the Great Beyond and leave us on the dark shores of sorrow. . . ." Figurative language flirts with artificiality when overdone. On this point Longinus is emphatic:

> The cunning use of figures arouses a peculiar suspicion in the hearer's mind, a feeling of being deliberately trapped and misled. . . . That is why the best use of a figure is when the . . . figure goes unnoticed.

Longinus adds that "cunning techniques, when overlaid with beauty and passion, disappear from view." The advice still applies to writers, who must be cunning to craft dramatic literary effects—and then doubly cunning to hide the effort. Here are two figurative descriptions of celebrities. The first fails to hide its figures, which are too heavy-handed to be forceful. The second, in spite of an outlandish metaphor, is so passionate as to seem natural.

> On James Dean: "The wordless fury and hurt of abandonment were the scrap metal that Dean alchemized into cinematic gold, prophetically creating a mold for adolescent angst for years to come."[4]

> On Marlene Dietrich: "The cool bright face that didn't ask for anything, that simply existed, waiting—it was an empty face, . . . a face that could change with any wind of expression. One could dream into it anything. It was like a beautiful empty house waiting for carpets and pictures. It had all possibilities—it could become a palace or a brothel."[5]

A fresh figure helps get a message across, grabbing attention and animating the message. But too much figure and it drowns the message in associations. No writer (especially not this one) is innocent of "taking a metaphor to the gates of doom," as the critics say. After all, comparisons are natural and irresistible. Once a basic association is established such as A = B (e.g., life = a river), everything about A seems to fit some aspect of B. To stop after a perfect match or two is the mark of a pro; but even E. B. White in *The Elements of Style* could be drawn into five or more: "The language . . . is a living stream, shifting, changing, receiving new strength from a thousand tributaries, losing old forms in the backwaters of time. To suggest that a young writer not swim in the main stream of this turbulence would be foolish indeed. . . ."

Less Is More

As much as overworked figures diminish force, understatement can drive a message through granite. "Less is more" is law in the arts, because less allows an audience to make its own discoveries and thus share the excitement of creativity. But "less" has to trail enough clues to give the audience a direction. When someone drawls, "Interesting dress," we have to know that the dress in question is open to the navel. In Kazuo Ishiguro's *The Remains of the Day* we know how desperately a repressed English butler wants to cry out, "I abandoned my dying father to serve fools, and my whole life has been a bloody lie!" Instead, his mannered style grows increasingly understated:

> . . . if you consider the pressures contingent upon me that night, you may not think I delude myself unduly if I go so far as to suggest that I did perhaps display, in the face of everything, at least in some modest degree a "dignity" . . .[6]

Restraint is a gift to our audiences; it says, "I only have to hint at what I mean, and I can count on you to make the forceful connections." One type of restraint is to offer a *telling detail* to stimulate a response, rather than (as in the left column, following) tell the audience what to feel:

Will was the kind of offbeat and engaging child who loved wonton soup and studied the fishlike wontons with the precocious interest that brings both elation and existential anxiety to a mother's heart.

"Will loved wonton soup. He loved the special spoon that came with it and had as much interest in the wontons sunk to the bottom as a fisherman looking at trout in clear water." (Ann Beattie, *Picturing Will*, Random House, 1989)

Macon pulled into a service station, so depressing in the rain, and cut off the engine as if it were his whole past life. He rubbed his knees in sad, tongue-tied desperation. Sarah drew away miserably. The only sound was the heartbreaking drumming of the rain on the overhang above them.

"He pulled into a Texaco station, parked beneath the overhang, and cut off the engine. Then he started rubbing his knees with his palms. Sarah huddled in her corner. The only sound was the drumming of the rain on the overhang far above them." (Anne Tyler, *The Accidental Tourist*, Knopf, 1985)

Figures of Gab

As in creative writing, we use rhetorical figures constantly in everyday expression. Most of these figures go unnoticed, not because we overlay them with beauty and passion but because they are ordinary, overworked, or both. To achieve impact we would need to ratchet up our conversational figures, not to the point of cunningness but enough to make them fresh and distinctive.

How common is figurative language? It is impossible to stick to the literal in any extended communication. Thoughts themselves may be densely figurative associations that we partially strip down into statements. Whole cultures and subcultures wrap themselves in certain figures. In New York City, *irony* is an institution; statements mean their opposite: "I love waiting an hour to get served. Remind me to come here every night." The English favor understatement. "Bit of an inconvenience, this," says the quadriplegic British war veteran. And Churchill: "I have not had an uneventful life."

One has only to examine a chunk of conversation to see how classical figures—from the familiar to the most arcane—are represented. Even the word *like,* the epidemic American interjection, can be seen as a form of *simile* in certain uses: "And I'm like, eeeyoo, get away from me!" (i.e., I am like someone in a situation saying "Eeeyoo, get away from me!"). Following is a casual exchange between acquaintances Laurie and Margaret, meeting in a pub. What sounds unaffected to us in their chatter approximates some of the most deliberate figurative forms (named at right) of the classical rhetoricians. Of the two women, who is the more expressive?

Is that you, Laurie? You must be ecstatic to see me. Want a handkerchief?

Irony: Clearly meaning the opposite of what is said.

Oh, hi, Margaret. I'm a wreck, I guess. But I'm not really crying.

Metaphor: A comparison implied by direct attribution. Laurie *is* a "wreck," therefore very much *like* a wreck.

No, your eyes always look like strawberry margaritas. What's up?

Simile: An explicit comparison, using *like, as,* or *as if.*

Don't ask.

Significatio: Signifying more than one says.

I hope it's some delicious torment.

Oxymoron: Pairing of two incongruous or contradictory terms.

I'd tell you, but the walls have ears.

Prosopopoeia or Personification: Endowing human attributes to something inanimate or abstract.

Laurie! Are you seeing that married Lothario again?

Epiplexis: Questioning as a form of reproach. **Allusion:** Brief reference to a widely familiar person, place, or happening.

So? I'm lonely. I'm depressed. I have low self-esteem. I'm no spring chicken.

Threnos: Lamentation, a litany of hardships. **Litotes:** Affirming by negating (she is no young fowl, so she must be an old one), a form of understatement.

And he's no capon. I hear he's chasing every skirt in town.

Synecdoche: Using a part (skirt) to signify the whole (woman). Or **Metonymy:** Using an attribute of something as a name for it.

I knew that—no, I didn't. Tell me what else you've heard. No, don't.

Epanorthosis: Correcting or pulling back on a statement.

Oh, I wouldn't. It's not for me to say that he's a wife-beater.

Apophasis: Mentioning by denying mention.

My ignorance is bliss. Besides, he's too good for her. He could

Paradox: A seemingly absurd or contradictory statement that

have married anyone. He felt sorry for her.

Yes, Laurie, he's a trophy. A rare gift to women. We thank the gods for men like him.

I admit he's no saint.

Saint? Someone who hunks himself around like rent-a-meat?

Well, anyway, he says it's over. Adios. Finito. End of story.

Oh Lord, give this girl some gray matter! How many times has he fed you that line? Listen to some sage advice: "It ain't over till it's over." Save your self-respect and drop him like the putrefied piece of women-hating waste matter that he is. Get your life together. Start appreciating the exceptional person that you are. And pass me one of those pretzels.

makes sense. **Eulogia:** Extended praise.

Sarcasm: Scornful language, here praise that condemns. **Diasyrm:** Sly put-down as in mocking praise.

Litotes: See above.

Anthimeria, or **Enallage:** Using one part of speech as another (the noun hunk as a verb) for effect. **Simile:** See above.

Commoratio: Emphasizing a point by repeating it in different terms.

Invocation: Calling upon a higher power. **Metonymy:** "Gray matter for brain"—see definition above. **Apomnemonysis:** Quoting a respected authority. **Bdelygmia:** A stream of abuse, of denunciation. **Euphemism:** A mild term ("waste matter") for a more offensive one. **Catacosmesis:** Statements in descending order of importance, sometimes ending in the trivial for anticlimax.

Learning to Be Deviant

If figurative language had never been heard on earth, almost any deviation from the literal would excite the multitudes. I could say, "Free enterprise is the cornerstone of democracy" and be nominated for President. But English has been shaped by more than twelve hundred years of figurative deviations. Flight from the literal tends to land one squarely on a worn-out figure.

When is a figure worn out? When it no longer projects its association. Such figures as "eye of a needle" are called "dead metaphors." "Faded metaphors" are those that are half-dead. An example: "They ran like crazy to keep up with the whirlwind tour." Did the forces of madness or cyclonic winds come to mind? On hearing "I need this like a hole in the head," are we picturing a bloody crater in the center of one's brow? No, we perceive only the message "I don't need this."

To be forceful, then, we must be dedicated deviants, relying on (1) inventiveness, (2) use of deviant expression not yet heard by our audience, and (3) prompts from language reference works such as thesauri and specialized word collections.

Inventiveness begins when we dispatch the cliché figures that flock like zombies toward our every sentence. We are then forced to replace them with something live. Reference works abound to help us recognize and zap clichés. Some of these guides, like *Thesaurus of Alternatives to Worn-Out Words and Phrases* by Robert Hartwell Fiske (Writer's Digest Books, 1994), suggest replacements for the terms they list. Before checking with Fiske, I might have said, "A forceful figure is one that is *a breed apart,* or *a breed unto itself."* Fiske would replace that cliché with one of the following durable terms: aberrant, anomalous, atypical, eccentric, singular, unorthodox—or several other alternatives. Any one of these would make the point, though not as memorably as an apt image. "A forceful figure is one that rides in like a masked avenger." Any better? You try.

Avoiding overworked patterns even with the help of reference books and software does not suddenly empower one's language. Nor does the invention of figures that are off-target or too arcane for the audience. To hype a recent novel by Umberto Eco, the author's publisher proclaimed: "It's like a Dumas story written by Pascal." Millions were uncaptivated. Empowerment comes from precision, precision, precision; from language that harpoons the exact meaning, the nuance, for the intended audience. Literary theory holds that a precise figure not only clarifies your experience to an audience, but helps the audience arrange experience in a coherent and aesthetic pattern. This is power.

Faded metaphors do not capture nuance. Consider "happy as a clam." Used as early as 1800, the figure might once have distinguished a precise, mollusky shade of serenity from general exultation as in "happy as a lark." By the time it came into wide use, the phrase had grown to "happy as a clam at high tide," meaning safe (from clammers) or about as happy as a commuter back in the suburbs; not very special. "Happy as a clam" now signals nothing.

Exactly how happy are *you*? This is a subtle matter and no one expects a literal answer. Happy as a hippo in a hot tub? Happy as anchovy paste? Happy as a fury with her hair on fire? You need figures all your own. Luckily there are millions of images out there (including those within clichés), waiting for new and deviant uses. To find them is more a matter of tenacity than brilliance. Take it from Mr. *Sublime* himself:

> We have had sufficient proof that a good many writers of prose and poetry who have no natural genius—often, indeed, no great inborn talent—use commonplace, popular words, and as a rule, no unusual language; yet, by the mere arrangement and harmonizing of these words they endow their work with dignity, distinction, and the appearance of not being ordinary.
> —Cassius Longinus

9

Make My Day:
The Power of Tough Talk

*T*ough talk is a style of putting antisocial and protective thoughts into words. It seeks to relieve the speaker's anxiety even at the expense—often gleefully at the expense—of those on the receiving end.

Thought: *I want this person to go away and not come back soon.* Words: Kiss off. Piss off. Buzz off. Shove off. Beat it. Take a powder. Go take your shoes for a walk.

While not everyone's first idiom, tough talk comes in handy when the going gets tough. And whose going ever gets easier? When life isn't a scramble for survival, it's hard cheese or nasty bits or someone on your back or in your face or at your throat. *So get your mind around it, sucker. World ain't no drawing room. Ain't no debate club. Eye for a tooth, pal. What'd Capone say? "You get fadda widda kind word and a gun den widda kind word alone." Believe it! You want to jet with your life, you got to kill with words. Poolroom, boardroom, don't matter. Tough talk be the power.*

You got a problem with that?

Every society develops tough expression, more or less apart from its forms of civil (considerate) discourse. And such expression seems to be getting tougher by the minute; crueler, more eruptive, more menacing than ever before. Outrage and rancor are among the virtues of the day. Yet antisocial expression is probably as old as human rivalry, not always the stuff of history but surely present and dirt-mean from the start. And now that the mass-media and entertainment industries have bulldozed it from the background of culture to the foreground, we are buried in it. We wallow in it. Revel in it.

Toughness may be no tougher than ever, but today everyone is talking the talk. Men, women, clergy, academics, administrators, heads of state, everyone. They are doing so because, often enough, tough talk is socially acceptable, attention-getting, stimulating, entertaining. It feels good to unload, and it zaps adversaries. The zapping idiom floods the media, from the business and sports sections to the editorial pages. An executive of Id Software (maker of the video game Doom) describes his colleagues as "into the stick the shotgun in your mouth and blow the back of your skull off kind of software."[1] Op-ed columnist Anna Quindlen writes that "Newt Gingrich goes straight for the neck flesh, calling names, talking trash, practicing his patented brand of 'I'm-O.K.-You're-Scum' attack politics."[2]

Tough talk gets under our skin. It grates against tranquillity. But as a medium for expressing our own hurts and aggressions, it soothes us where we seethe. We love its energy and defiance. Compared to most of our sterile blather, it can be high expression—and, up to a point, easier to adapt than literary forms. And so we embrace it and make it ours. And we dish it out to the next SOB who steps on our toes.

A Definition

Tough talk, our final topic under "extrusions," I define broadly as any expression armored against vulnerability. It is a growl, not only aggressive but protective—words not to be squooshed, squelched, or deflated. It is hard-ass, if not always kick-ass. Rhett Butler's "Frankly, my dear, I don't give a damn" was tough talk, protecting Rhett's pride and flapping the unflappable Scarlett. In 1939 producer David O. Selznik had to butt heads with Hollywood censors to retain the line rather than the suggested "Frankly, my dear, I don't care." Scarlett would have mashed those words back in Rhett's kisser.

Other notable tough lines show the steel plating of literal thoughts:

Why not give me an excuse to shoot you legally, an act I would find satisfying?	"Go ahead, make my day." (Clint Eastwood, *Sudden Impact)*
Vacate the space you are occupying so that I might enter it.	"Make a hole, pal." (Don Johnson, *Miami Vice)*
I am about to inflict upon you perhaps the first bleeding wound you've had in a very long while.	"How long has it been since you've had a real hemorrhage?" (Dianne Wiest, *Bullets over Broadway)*
I favor a degree of intellectual weakness in men with whom I have a relationship.	"You're not too bright. I like that in a man." (Kathleen Turner, *Body Heat)*
I'd prefer it if you didn't volunteer your opinions.	"When I want your advice, I'll beat it out of you." (Chuck Norris, *Code of Silence)*
Rise, you unpleasant person.	"Get up, you scum-suckin' pig." (Marlon Brando, *One-Eyed Jacks)*

Literal expression can be tough in its own right, just as we've seen it to be forceful in other ways. The challenge "You talking to *me?*" is literal yet armored. As figurative language, tough talk stretches meanings and stimulates the imagination. "Leave me alone" means only what it says. But "Get out of my face" is a figurative expression with a hundred shades of meaning, depending on the situation. It uses *synecdoche,* or the part (face) to stand for the whole (person). Almost any of the rhetorical devices (see last chapter) can be used to armor expression. For example:

Hyperbole: When I'm through with you, you'll be on so much ice you'll think you're a chilled vermouth.
Understatement (litotes): I am not a nice lady when double-crossed.
Metonymy: They'll need ten uniforms to collar that doll.
Sarcasm: Let's go for a ride, pretty boy. You'll love the scenery.
Rhetorical question: What do I look like, some bimbo?
Metaphor: Tell your gorillas I got a job for 'em.
Simile: I'll be on you like white on rice.
Enallage: Ungrateful? Ungrateful *this!* I'll ungrateful *you!*

Toughness, like all effects, can be a matter of precision—of picking words that hit the bull's-eye in nuance and sound. "I ask for drop-dead handsome, I get this plug-ugly mutt!" Hardness comes also from syntax (word order) or grammatical patterns used by tough groups and individuals. The present-habitual tense of "to be" is now part of Standard American Kid-lish: "Yo, I be telling you, Ma, don't be puttin' no carrot in my lunchbox." And toughness comes from deft use of slang, that loopy lexicon, that "language with an attitude" of which we shall say more later.

Varieties of Tough Talk

Tough talk includes the profane, hurtful, shocking, and threatening—the stuff of an average minute in Brooklyn—as well as all the world's more sophisticated malediction.[3] At the high end one would have to at least consider the Bible's wrathful words and curses, including those of God in such passages as "The Prophesies Against Foreign Nations" (Ezekiel 29:3–6):

> See! I am coming at you, Pharaoh, king of Egypt . . . who say, "The Niles are mine; it is I who made them!" I will put hooks in your jaws and make the fish of your Niles stick to your scales, then draw you up from the midst of your Niles along with all the fish of your Niles sticking to your scales. I will cast you into the desert, you and all the fish of your Niles. . . .[4]

But even when aggressive and abusive, God's words fall outside my definition of tough talk; they need no armoring against vulnerability. Many on Earth, however, strive for Godlike diction in castigating their enemies. Our politicians and CEOs favor this tone: "Your bankrupt and insensitive outburst shames every hardworking citizen of this great nation and casts a pall on decency itself." Lawyers, if not always Godlike, are trained rhetoricians and adept at many levels of invective. Geoffrey Fieger, attorney for "suicide doctor" Jack Kevorkian, illustrates part of the range when he calls the Michigan governor "a truly goofy, stupid man, certifiably evil" and a county judge "a vile, malignant, legal lunatic."[5]

Forceful as it may be, such American malediction is small change next to the vitriol of Third World revolutionaries and of older societies. A Peruvian linguist recently observed how the Shining Path rebel movement "uses words like bullets," calling its enemies "animal generals with worm-eaten brains" and the President of Peru "the genocidal hyena, whom we will frontally combat until we see him crushed like the filthy and obscene rat that he is." More subtle but no less scathing is the tough talk of Mandarin Chinese, poetic in its imagery. An offensive young upstart whom we would call a "punk" is dubbed "rǔ-còu wèi-gān" in Mandarin, literally "milk stink not dry."[6] Hollywood needs lines like that. For example, *Carlito's Way* is a tough-talking film in which ex-con Carlito (Al Pacino) tells a young rival, "You ain't like me. You a punk." Now for the tougher rewrite: "You ain't like me, punk. You milk stink not even dry."

For all its malignancy, tough talk can also deliver benign messages in certain contexts. "Break a leg, you stagestruck idiot," is a good wish in a tough casing. Tough talk can be directed to one's self, but the flagellation is meant to beat others to the punch, roughen the surface. The gumshoe greets the day with a bracing self-assault: "When I came to I looked like I'd spent the night with a kinky taxidermist. . . ."

The Bad Words

Lately, the lower depths of public expression seem bottomless. In motion pictures, cable programming, and prime-time broadcasting, profanity is as common as cornflakes. And yet Americans by the millions still get offended; even "broad-minded" individuals have quirky areas of offense-taking. So-called gutter speech or taboo language is still hot-wired, to be handled with care whether plugged into insult, comedy, or art. Before I use vulgar or shocking language, and I sometimes do, I weigh the intended effects against unwanted results. Is the usage appropriate in the situation or absurd? Is it creative, witty, or trite and dumb? Will it shock? Offend? Do I want to shock and offend? Offend the whole audience or part? Will offense suit my purpose or defeat it? How big and mean is the offended object?

The remainder of this chapter contains some profanity. Considering the range of tastes among people interested in language, I chose to soften the most taboo terms with asterisks. Readers who feel they might be offended anyway may wish to proceed to the next chapter, though I promise no worse than what explodes in Dolby stereo each weekend at your neighborhood multiplex.

•   •   •

Anyone with ears knows that tough talk in America is driven by two words above all others: sh*t and f*ck, along with their derivatives. C*ck, pr*ck, and c*nt aren't far behind. And the behind itself, under several names, gets kicked, whupped, beat, broken, and otherwise abused and invaded in a thousand tough expressions. It is entirely possible to tough-talk without the most vulgar terms; thousands of tough characters did so in films and literature until World War II. But partly as a result of the war and its diffusion of previously taboo language, these vulgarities are the terms that most armor American speech, that clang through our tirades and even casual complaints, that intensify our verbal attacks and defenses.

Author and amateur linguist Anthony Burgess devotes a chapter to "Low-Life Language" in *A Mouthful of Air,* his observations on English. Here he reviews the etymology of sh*t from a probable Indo-European root *skheid,* meaning to split or divide, by way of similar German, Norse, Dutch, and Old English words for excrement. "It is understandable," he says, "that the excretory terms should be used in contexts of contempt, dislike, pain. . . ."[7]

It is understandable as well that sh*t permeates tough talk, where the offensiveness of excrement keeps the enemy at bay. Sh*t is a universal anxiety reliever—often the word of choice to express sudden pain or fear. In tough talk it is a formidable anxiety *giver,* as when applied to someone's brains, head, face, or general insides; or to their arguments, work, or ways. The word might well be the most common metaphor in American tough talk, an armored stand-in for any entity under the sun and for the sun itself: "Hey, move that sh*t into the warehouse." "You better get your sh*t together, man." "He be dealing some good sh*t." "Baby, you'll have diamonds, furs, all that sh*t." "Stay outta the sun; that sh*t'll give you cancer."

The F-Word

The word f*ck intrigues Burgess, who notes that, like sh*t, it is an ancient word that civilization has shunned more out of "social decorum" than mindless repression. Squeamishness about these words and others with sexual and excretory referents goes back a long way, he says. He does not mention, however, how quickly young children take to such terms; apparently squeamishness is relearned each generation. At about age three, one of my daughters constructed the curiously powerful admonition "Go make a f*ck in your pants." I had, ahem, no idea where she had heard the f-word; but hers was an unsqueamish application of what she knew to be an attention-getting utterance—and a risky negative one.

The f-word retains its negative potency into adulthood, even if no one has explained to Burgess's satisfaction why "the most pleasurable activity known to mankind, and the organs by which it is procured, should be debased . . . as expressions of opprobrium." Actually, opprobrium seems reasonable given the negative takes on sex even today—as sin, as disease, as war between man and woman, as political liability. A keener mystery is why f*ck has so embedded itself in late-twentieth-century expression, why it has become the putt-putt of verbal engines from the mean streets to the corridors of power. Has it risen on the decline of other middle-class-toughness manifestations—of speakeasies, fat cigars, cigarettes dangling from the lips, fedoras pulled over the eyes? Is f*ck simply the most perfectly armored sound utterable? Whatever the reason, it is a word that, linguistically speaking, is enjoying phenomenal success after at least five hundred years in the English language.

Not only is the f-word ubiquitous in national expression, but its grammatical flexibility allows it a place in any sentence we can construct. Burgess recalls a motor mechanic, perhaps British, who in one outburst over a balky engine used the word in five distinct parts of speech: "F*ck it, the f*cking f*cker's f*cking f*cked." When Americans get going—especially to impress tough-talking peers—they can caulk an entire narrative with the word, working it into every grammatical crevice and jamming it between syllables as an infix—"unf*ckingbelievable!"[8]

Sometimes, as in moments of rage, one finds no intensifier more appropriate, none more "correct" in the sense of suiting the situation. Consider this quiz: An acquaintance was to meet you at nine and shows up, without apologizing, after you have waited for one hour and thirty-three minutes in the frigid cold. What is the correct time to report to the acquaintance? (a) ten-thirty-three (b) ten-f*cking-thirty-three (c) ten-f*cking-thirty-f*cking-three (d) f*cking ten-f*cking-thirty-f*cking-three!

The stature of f*ck in American expression is documented in the *Random House Historical Dictionary of American Slang,* a massive and widely heralded reference work whose first volume, *A–G,* appeared in 1994. Out of some twenty thousand entries in the volume, more than eighty describe terms beginning with f*ck and offer lush and often amusing examples from print, manuscript, broadcast, and other collected sources. A meager sampling:

"Both were serious f*ckaholics."
"That was an act of pure human f*ckery."
"F*cking-ay-John Ditty-Bag-well-told I don't."
"Do me one more favor, Private. Dis-a-f*ckin'-pear!"

Twelve jumbo pages of this dictionary, packed with variations and examples, celebrate America's love affair with the feisty little sound of an *f* and an *uh* and a *k*.[9]

Using Tough Talk

Prisoners, drug dealers, and members of other subcultures develop informal codes for use of their lingos, but few rules can be applied to tough talking in general. You use it when you believe an audience will respond to it. You may be giving tit for tat, or armoring your expression to protect yourself. In speaking, the one general rule is to stay in character—stretch your natural expression into tough talk that fits you, not someone else. If you are developing a new and tougher self, it may be wise to do so in stages.

Some time ago I joined a neighborhood bowling league in Chicago, where tough talk was rampant. It was raunchy, mocking, and crudely aggressive. The bowlers, most of them in the construction trades, were working off steam. For two or three seasons I tried imitating the prevailing style. *Hey, gimmee the buck, jagoff, whaddyoo got fishhooks in your pocket? So I duke this scumbag a fiver and still he gets smart—I shoulda put him in the hospital wearin' diapers.* But I was out of character and as a result had no character. My words vaporized into the smoky air. It wasn't until I settled on a bogus literary style—something like "Edward, go forth and bowl, Foul Spirit!"—that Eddie and the others took note: "Hey, you hear what this jagoff just said?"

In creative writing, the challenge is to find the right shade of toughness for narrator or character and make it sound authentic. Writers may hope to rely on ear and memory, thinking they have heard enough of the real thing to know its nuances. But often what they remember are the common profanities and not the words and structure that distinguish one brand of tough talk from another. Profanity becomes an art in itself.

It must ring true. It must be used with some restraint and purpose, even in representing the most unthinkingly foulmouthed characters. Used at length it must be colorful or dramatic or funny, not simply there for verisimilitude. It must not drive out other inventive uses of language.

Modern writers with a knack for elevating profanity to art include David Mamet, Richard Price, Martin Scorsese, Nicholas Pileggi, John Edgar Wideman, Quentin Tarantino, Erica Jong, and Joyce Carol Oates. Audiences of every social stripe, for example, listen adoringly when Mamet's characters spew lines such as these in *Glengarry Glen Ross:*

> What the f*ck, what bus did *you* get off of, we're here to f*cking *sell*. *F*ck* marshaling the leads. What the f*ck talk is that? What the f*ck talk is that? . . . what I'm saying is it's *f*cked.*[10]

Profanity suits Mamet's style of razor-sharp, ruthless give-and-take. His characters, as vulnerable as any, armor themselves in it. For an hour or two their outrageous tough talk is thrillingly ours.

Tough talk is a broader weapon for Scorsese. It is a verbal bludgeon wielded by murderous hoods, every bit as menacing as their guns and yet amusing (to many) in its expressiveness. In *GoodFellas,* written with Pileggi, the dialogue of one scene is so inventively tough that thousands of American moviegoers recite it as if it were the Pledge of Allegiance. Hotheaded killer Tommy (Joe Pesci) tests wise-guy-in-training Henry (Ray Liotta) by faking insult at an offhanded remark: Henry has called Tommy a "funny" storyteller. Tommy silences the barroom crowd and addresses a terrified Henry:

> You mean, let me understand this . . . I'm funny, how? I mean, funny like I'm a clown? I amuse you? I make you laugh. I'm here to f*cking amuse you. What do you mean

funny? Funny how? How am I funny? . . . You said I'm
funny. How the f*ck am I funny? What the f*ck is so funny
about me? Tell me. Tell me what's so funny. . . .[11]

In the novels and screenplays of Richard Price, tough talk
seems less crafted than simply transcribed from life—a tribute
to the author's craft as well as his ear for street vernacular.
"Price writes dialogue that rings as true as a slap across the
face," says a typical review *(Boston Globe)*. But no matter how
well Price hears the lingo and cadence of inner-city cops and
druggies, he must still shape language to distinguish one character from another, advance the plot, and maintain the novelty
by which he has engaged readers. One novelty in *Clockers,* a
saga of the juvenile drug trade, is an elaborate name-calling
style which in rhetorical terms would be simile or *bdelygmia*
(string of execrations):

> "Yeah? Let me tell you something, you E.T.-looking
> motherf*cker."
> ". . . they got me hands up on the car, this little old
> pink-eyed Santa Claus–looking motherf*cker patting me
> up my legs."
> "Yo, Thumper, you white, Pee Wee–looking mother-
> f*cker!"
> "You're a skinny-ass snake motherf*cker nobody-to-noth-
> ing piece of street sh*t."[12]

For a novelist, pervasive use of street dialect is a risk not to
be taken lightly; the terms can date in a matter of months.
Price is inventive enough to be durable. He also risks turf-
invasion as a white writer portraying black toughs and their
dialect, just as John Edgar Wideman, who is black, dares to
write as a Jew recalling the Holocaust, or Calcutta-born Bharati
Mukherjee as a male Iraqi-American hustler outhustling a murderous Texan in Mexico. Cross-cultural writing is nothing new,

but authors are often pressured to stay within their own milieu. As the world becomes more diversified, such restriction is ridiculous for any serious writer—in creating tough talk as well as any other effect. Tough talk belongs to no one group in particular; each subculture has its variety, each has contributed to the common store. What drives toughness, as much as those dialects we tend to associate with it, are such universal elements as:

Physical Menace. Especially harm to one's body or loved ones: "I'm gonna hang you like a side of beef. . . . I'm gonna pop your eyes like busted eggs. I'm gonna make your tongue stretch so far out you'll be lickin' your toes." (Jack "Legs" Diamond in William Kennedy's *Legs*). *I'll punch your lights out. I'll tear your face off. I'll hit you so hard I'll kill your whole family.* Verbs associated with such harm: *The President lacerated his critics.*

Dire Consequence. Threats, often unspecified, but based on one's power to deliver: *Don't mess with Texas.* "Ah'mo get medieval on yo' ass" (Ving Rhames about to torture his torturer in Tarantino's *Pulp Fiction*). "Say something smarter than that, Sipowitz; you're gonna be dead a long time" (to Dennis Franz, about to be shot on *NYPD Blue*). Joyce Carol Oates *(On Boxing,* Ecco, 1994) points out the ferociousness of boxers' ring names: The Manassa Mauler, Hands of Stone, Bonecrusher, Mad Dog, and Pit Bull.

Insult. Degradation that diminishes the target: "I swear, if you existed, I'd divorce you" (Liz Taylor, *Who's Afraid of Virginia Woolf?*). "I crap bigger than you" (Jack Palance, *City Slickers*).

Defiance. Resistance against law, convention, conquest, conformity, or other restraints: *Don't tread on me.* "My hat's in the ring. The fight is on and I'm stripped to the buff" (Theodore Roosevelt). "Sorry—floors don't feel good under my knees" (Vance Bourjaily, *Now Playing at Canterbury*). "A man can't ride your back unless it's bent" (Martin Luther King, Jr.). "I can't be a rose in any man's lapel" (Margaret Trudeau).

Slang: "Language with an Attitude"

Any style, high or low, can serve to express defiance. But a special body of language known as *slang* takes to the task like a band of juiced guerrillas. Although slang is used abundantly in this chapter and embraced throughout the book, we haven't stopped to say just what it is and what it does for expressiveness. Now, as we close our *rap* on tough talk, the time is short but *righteous*. We *cool* on that?

Slang is an army of rebel terms and phrases numbering perhaps a quarter million in America. Each term rebels against one or more Standard English equivalents, though in degrees ranging from playful to sociopathic. *Cracked* rebels against "mentally disturbed," *puss* against "face," *head honcho* against "chief executive," and so on to the ugly extremes such as *bitch* in defiance of the term "woman" or the most hate-driven racial epithets.

This vast sublanguage coexists and intermingles with Standard English, but never merges with it; when former slang terms such as *snob* or *jitters* become standard, they are no longer antiestablishment, no longer slang. Many—perhaps most—slang terms are standard words that have acquired additional, slang meanings; for example, the use of *nut* to mean cranium, testicle, insane person, enthusiast, payment, and so on. The slang meanings are generally more ephemeral than the standard, in and out of fashion; but many—such as those for *nut*—endure.

Slang and tough talk are bosom pals but not synonymous. Many applications of slang as well as whole subsets (jazz, hackerspeak, Wall Street, etc.) have little to do with armoring expression. Some slang terms are simply too charming or cute to be tough. A *dandy deb* from *Dixie* isn't the baddest image in town. Still, tough talk draws so heavily on slang for its rebelliousness that no aspiring tough talker can proceed without a good lexicon of slang at hand (see Resources).

J. E. Lighter, editor of the Random House slang dictionary (1994–) cited earlier, is Supreme Slang*meister* these days as he and his staff gather some 200,000 to 300,000 vivid examples of American slang to illustrate about 50,000 to 60,000 terms in three volumes scheduled for completion in 1997. Lighter distinguishes slang from what is simply new or informal in a language. He cites slang's irreverence, its "insider" quality, its pep, color, and personality; and he adds:

> Slang is raw, vital, ribald, and flip. It intimates an *in-your-face* attitude. . . . Many think that because so much slang centers on body functions, sex, insults, intoxication, money, criminal activity and the like, its use indicates deficiency of character or intelligence. More accurately, it's better to assume that those who use slang hold an antiestablishment attitude and display sharp disdain for convention and pretense.[13]

Sound like anyone you know, you rebel you? If you have spent any time in America, if you have ever said "Bull!" or "I don't care *beans* what people will think!" or worn some nasty T-shirt, you are already a user of American slang; you have used slangy tough talk to rebel against pretense and convention, to extrude thoughts, to protect yourself.

That doesn't mean you have done so brilliantly or are ready to be the next Elmore Leonard or Sara Paretsky. As with any new language, excellence in slang requires immersion, selectivity, inventiveness, and one more thing: a large set of those pendulous brass spheres (I believe there's a slang term) symbolizing the courage to take chances.

III

Patternings

Model Expression:
In Search of Paradigms

A century or more ago . . . if you *did* happen
to listen to a Lincoln, a Douglas, an Emerson,
a Robert Ingersoll, you heard language composed
and spoken well. The models were few—
not available to all. Today the models are many—
available to all—and not so good.
—Clifton Fadiman,
Britannica Book of English Usage

*N*ow and then in a B movie, aliens from outer space patch
together an instant Earthspeak based on the first models they
run across: *Check it out, Earthling, we gon borrow Dad's wheels and
bop to the hop.* Many Americans coming out of childhood do the
same. They seize upon the prevailing, generic models of expression before they can discern the more distinctive ones.
The common drives out the precise. To express the world
mainly in terms of "totally" this and "mind-blowing" that
seems almost a betrayal of human language ability, the miracle
that begins to unfold in our infancy.

Recent linguistic theory points to a "language instinct": an
inherited, hard-wired grammatical logic in the baby brain. As

toddlers we start to recognize the functions of words and word parts and categorize them accordingly. For example, we learn that "I" = thing that acts; "eat" = present action; and "—ed" = past action. With these tagged words in our database, we plug in our instinctive software and we make sentences: "I eated my supper." Logical and natural. Parents and others coach the child in exceptions to the logic ("*ate* my supper") and in language conventions they believe to be "correct" or standard within the culture.

Whether by language instinct or pure imitation, children up to age six show astounding natural ability to acquire new words and fit them to thoughts. But from then on, the new words come harder and the thoughts grow more complex. The expressive little geniuses have merely caught up to the masses of speaking organisms. Those who would extend their range and distinguish themselves must emulate the patterns of exemplary speakers and writers. These are the models, or paradigms, that shape expression.

Models tend to be composites of various patterns or styles. There is no single model of, say, poetic expression. An exemplary poetic style such as that of Derek Walcott's *Omeros* might be a mix of Standard English, classical echoes, slang, dialect, and so on. But each model has a certain dominant characteristic that invites imitation.

For the teaching of rhetoric, models are usually grouped by purpose: exposition, argument, description, and narration. Another way to divide them is by the "worlds" that supply the patterns we imitate. The main half-dozen categories might be: parental or home, academic, professional, commercial, literary or artistic, and popular. "Exemplary" expression within these overlapping groups and thousands of subgroups is entirely relative. Exemplary means a model that communicates in a style perfectly suited to one's ambitions.

John Kennedy's inaugural rhetoric represents one such paradigm:

. . . ask not what your country can do for you; ask what you can do for your country.

Boxer James "Quick" Tillis's pre-fight hype reflects another:

You gotta pay the cost to be the boss, and Tuesday night I'll be hot sauce.

And the high-fashion banter of *Vogue*'s André Leon Talley a third:

This collection is more divine than the last, . . . a high moment of Grecian simplicity, of fluted skirts in the material of a high rustling mega-moment, from room to room, à la the essence of King Louis XV, à la the true spirit of couture![1]

Three successful models for three types of ambition. A worthy model must help articulate thoughts or achieve desired effects. Ideally it does both. Certain paradigms are more seductive than others; they may be easier to imitate, fresher, hipper, more musical. But do they work for you? Noticing the patterns influencing your expression allows you a chance to reconsider them. Are they expanding your range or locking you into a type?

The Way They *Talk*

Most children emulate the parental (or home-caregiver) model until preteen hormones cause them to gag at the idea. For better or worse, the ways our parents spoke (reflecting all *their* models) reside within our own style for a lifetime and trickle down to the next generation. From mothers and fathers, we first acquire the general male and female models. No one has differentiated these models better than Deborah Tannen: Women express themselves to establish connections and negotiate relationships; men to preserve independence and negotiate and maintain status in a hierarchical social order.[2] We may try to suppress the parental models, but it is commonly observed that as people get older, they sound more than ever like their progenitors. *"You mind your manners, young lady—ohmigod, I sound just like Mom!"*

Those who were raised in well-spoken households may have no complaint, having received a gift that keeps giving—a way with words. One reads about literary families whose parlors buzzed with exquisite paradigms. Often a member of the clergy was on hand to contribute the celestial diction of the Word. What a supreme advantage—although its price may have been the suppression of useful "worldly" paradigms. For even as they emulate the home model, today's children tend to adopt the most atrocious (to parents) models in playground or schoolyard. "I ain't got to eat no yukky supper, so shut your stupid tushy-face!" they rasp, as if some reptilian instinct were kicking in. And it probably is, as a survival mechanism. In a crowded world the fittest individuals may be those who communicate successfully with the broadest range of human beings, whether to sell something, instill fear, or make babies.

The Uplifted Pupil

Traditional education has favored the society's "elevated" or "superior" models of expression. Exposed to a canon of so-called classics, a student might rise to the standard of the literate elite—even if some of the models are laughably archaic. But at least the classics serve as touch-points among the elite, a common language and shorthand for expressive discourse. If Julia says, "Art is long and time is fleeting," Jonathan gets it.

The challenge of reaching learners from every conceivable background has inspired broader approaches and, in recent times, a shift from "dead-white-male" paradigms to those more in tune with student passions. Too much liberal "reform," however, and the chaos of student-driven curricula stirs traditionalists to battle. Schools reinstitute "core" models, "back-to-basics" paradigms, programs of "cultural literacy" as defined by the cultures in power. Even as the nation moves from the "melting pot" concept of ethnic blending to the "salad bowl" of distinct subcultures, the yearning for a core is still heard. The core of a salad, if you can imagine it.

Standard English serves, more or less, as a national model for formal expression. But there can be no core model of expressiveness in America, one that everyone recognizes as worth emulating. There is no revered "King's English"; instead, the widely heard English of Stephen King, B. B. King, M. L. King, Billie Jean King, and Don King are among the styles that shape the national idiom. "Only in America could a Don King happen," says boxing promoter Don King in a typical utterance; and in another, "I never cease to amaze myself. I say this humbly."

We have no King's English, we have no presidential standard, even if certain presidents provide reliable patterns for mockery. What we do have as a resource are thousands of expressive styles, many of them ephemeral, but each with its appropriate uses. The Jewish style. The Soul style. The Salsa style. The Hollywood style. Executive. Preppie. Techie. Potomac. Wall Street. Deejay. Hip-hop. Gangsta. Uptown. Downtown. Are they all models of expression? *De facto*, yes, even if language guardians halt some of them at the borders.

In his *Paradigms Lost* (Potter, 1980), critic John Simon denies the legitimacy of any models other than those of Standard English. He does allow for individual style that is "flavorous, pungent, alive," but always *"within the framework of accepted grammar, syntax, and pronunciation."* Foreign born, Simon cites the Martian novels of Edgar Rice Burroughs as models he used in learning English, which is as wild and crazy as Simon gets. As for ethnic-American expression, he "submits" that: ". . . an English improvised by slaves and other strangers to the culture . . . under dreadfully deprived conditions, can nowise equal an English that the best literary and linguistic talents have, over the centuries, perceptively and painstakingly brought to a high level of excellence.''

So much for Simon's framework. For social mobility and public communications, there is no denying the value of Standard English and the importance of its model practitioners. But American expressiveness draws little from today's most common use of such English: the homogenized, cautious, and wooden language of the professional world, as in this sample:

> A policy on which to base practice is necessary. It is just as necessary that it be developed and written with the full participation of the paraprofessional staff, though these staff members have not previously been involved in articulating and formulating policy.

The vitality of American English is not here, not in news-hour reporting, not in the standard informational English by which Americans are processed from crib to coffin. The strength of ''American'' is in the diversity of its models from Hillbilly to Harvard and the democratic embrace in which we hold them all.

When we embrace the weakest elements of each model, however—the sloppy, the lazy, the mindless, and the stale—we speak American at its worst.

Mid-twentieth-century curricula in language and literature acknowledged the nation's diversity; today's offerings cover the cultural spectrum. In some educational programs, nonstandard patterns are credited as legitimate within their communities and worthy of attention. Even so, there remains visceral tension between the Standard English models and the vernacular and dialects in which students communicate. These variations of English, lively as they might be, cannot be supported as the language of mainstream communications or middle-class success. Most teachers feel they must bring about some movement toward the mainstream; if the students cannot be motivated to use Standard English, perhaps they can at least be trained to interpret and appreciate it.

Educators have been at that task for some time. Among old textbooks I scavenge now and then is a 1913 tome entitled *Natural Drills in Expression,* by Arthur Edward Phillips, principal of the Phillips School of Oratory in Chicago. A dedicated teacher of public speaking, Phillips had suffered long enough listening to students as they plodded through their readings of classic models. As he explained in his introduction:

> We set before the student . . . lines from Tennyson and ask him to read them. What a miserable failure he [the student] makes! Why? Because he is asked to give spontaneous expression to the thoughts and feelings of another, couched in words, style, and arrangement *foreign to his experience.* . . . Hence, he flounders through it in a manner that would make Tennyson weep.[3]

Phillips had a solution, and it had worked so well in his classrooms over the years that he could now reveal it in his book of "Tone Drills." Here he presented hundreds of bite-sized, classical models of superior expression, arranged by the emotional tone they represented, such as "gayety" or "awe." With these he paired what he described as "colloquial" models expressing the same emotion, but based on *student-related experience* and expressed in the *natural language of the student.* An example:

BOLDNESS:

Colloquial
Whether I get thrashed for it or not, I'll go right up to the teacher and tell her what I think of her.

Classical
Let it fall . . . though the fork invade
The region of my heart.
—Shakespeare, *King Lear, I, i*

Phillips claimed that his students, now feeling the "zest of true states" by expressing the familiar, no longer dreaded recitations; instead they could barely wait to be called upon. And it was probably true, even if his examples of "colloquial" student expression are as quaint today as ours will be tomorrow. Here are some of those down-to-earth colloquialisms he collected:

> **Reproof:** That was very ungentlemanly indeed.
> **Recklessness:** I don't care the snap of a finger whether I break my neck or not.
> **Joy:** Throw up your caps! We've won! Hurrah!

Teachers today practice a variation of the technique, using both homemade and published retellings of classics in student dialects. This can be done skillfully or in a way that makes people hate the idea. (*To check in or check out—that be the hang-up, dude.*) Shoe-horning the classics into student experience may lead to conceptual growth, but it will not extend the expressive range unless, somehow, the students are lured to the classics as paradigms. Here is where the art of teaching comes in: motivating students to cross cultures and to explore the possibilities of language.

A related approach is to provide exemplary models of excellence within a dialect, even to treat that dialect as a complex and systematic language of its own. In 1994 the American Bible Society published a bilingual English-Gullah edition of the New Testament Gospel. Next to each passage in King James English is a translation into Gullah, the African-English spoken by some quarter-million people of the southern Atlantic coast. "The Gospel According to Luke" becomes "De Good Nyews

Bout Jedus Christ Wa Luke Write." The King James's "He is not here, but is risen," translates into "Jedus ain't yah. E done git op from mongst de ded, an e da libe gin!"'—certainly more expressive to the community than the King's English, and not without sweetness to Anglo-English-trained ears.

At about the same time the African American Family Press published *Black Bible Chronicles,* a version geared to street-talking youngsters that somehow seems to have missed the richest nuances of street vernacular. The third and ninth commandments:

- You shouldn't dis the Almighty's name, using it in cuss words or rapping with one another. It ain't cool, and payback's a monster.
- Don't mess around with someone else's ol' man or ol' lady.

Ours was hardly the first society with tension between its formal and popular, or vernacular, models. That tension is universal. Infiltration of popular expression into formal usage is what shapes successful (adaptable) languages. Writers speed that process when they interface the formal and vernacular, playing one off the other. Here Philip Roth muses over the *pipik*—the Yiddish word for navel:

> Exactly what was your pipik trying to tell you? Nobody could ever really figure it out. You were left with only the word, the delightful playword itself, the sonic prankishness of the two syllabic pops and the closing click encasing those peepingly meekish, unobtrusively shlemielish twin vowels.[4]

Breaking the Mold

America is fraught with stock patterns, well-worn phrasing sustained by national leaders, the mass media, the professions. Some of these patterns have names, such as legalese, psychobabble, or jockese. You know them when you hear them:

> I gotta tell you, I was in the zone and right now I feel pretty stoked, you know, to be up there with the all-time greats because maybe you have some God-given talent but you don't get to be Number One without hard work and discipline and determination and the will to act in a positive way to achieve your personal best and pay your debt to all the people who support you so you can play your own game and never look back.

Can you smell the sweat? Although some athletes are perfectly articulate, even poetic, those who feed out the longest string of sports clichés seem to get the most exposure. One-dimensional golfers, ball players, tennis stars—together they may constitute the nation's most persistent model. (Why are athletes interviewed, anyway? Do we ask wordsmiths to run the bases?) Like most pop patter, jockese is infectious to those with low resistance—youngsters and non-native learners of the language. Unfortunately, most of it misses the simple grace achieved by a native Venezuelan, Manny Trillo, who played All Star second base for the Chicago Cubs and spoke like this:

> When you are hitting well, you want to think of nothing else. Not only is it pleasant to contemplate the memory and feel of success, but it is also useful to think of what you are doing right. But when things go wrong, you must forget all about it. You must not harp on what you have been doing wrong. You must go home and have a beer and watch television, and when . . . [someone] says, "Tomorrow's another day," you must nod your head as if those words contained all the wisdom in the world.[5]

Good reading offers escape from stock patterns. Writers can take the time to bring power and precision to words; readers can linger over those words and absorb them. But this is not to suggest a flight from all nonprint media, not even from mass media such as television. In fact, people who shun this source miss certain contemporary points of reference. Perhaps you have tried to establish rapport with a television teetotaler:

"Well, I'm eager to meet She Who Must Be Obeyed."

"Who?"

"Your wife. You know, as in *Rumpole? Rumpole of the Bailey?*"

"Is that a television thing? Sorry. We moved out here to watch the trees, not the tube."

Broadcast media offer stimulating as well as deadening models of expression. The tricks are to (1) stick to the most original shows and (2) pay attention to the language before it evaporates. Keep your journal handy. Joseph Campbell proved that talking heads can enthrall if the head utters old truths or fresh ideas in stimulating language. Julia Child turned a *bon mot* as gingerly as she whipped a souffle. Good words, engaging patterns pop up on *Star Trek, The Simpsons, The MacNeil/Leher NewsHour,* and, on radio, *All Things Considered, Prairie Home Companion,* and many more.

Somehow these well-exposed paradigms have not broken the mold of generic Americanese. Instead, American idiom is more reflective of talk-show schlock ("I guess your marriage partner just has to get in touch with his feelings, you know, deal with his hurt in terms of recovery before he can respect you as a person and get on with his life?") and of other uninventive patterns, such as body-workout banter ("It's great for my glutes, too!"). An enormous exercise facility I pass each evening has a glass facade that reveals scores of people working feverishly on their glutes (gluteus muscles, or butts). Soon they will all have identical butts as well as identical patter. But this is their choice, and so be it. Not everyone wants to build verbal sinew in precious spare hours.

Models, Muscular and Atrophied

Paradigms go through their own cycles of strength and decline. Most tired-out patterns enjoyed a potent youth, when qualities such as novelty, symbolism, precision, or status gave them muscle. Because they were powerful they were used often, used by everyone, used carelessly—until overuse atrophied every quality that once distinguished them. Even the all-purpose adjective "great," now a limp intensifier, had muscle in its precise Old English use as "coarse" or "gritty." Or imagine the first time in history that an annual report concluded: "We are well positioned to meet the future head-on." This new image would have evoked a heroic phalanx leveraging its might in the interests of shareholders. Now the words bid you to call your broker and sell.

Below are a few (actual) patterns of contemporary expression. Some may be odious to the discriminating ear, yet each represents a model that suits a certain ambition—until the intended audience tires of it and fresher paradigms bump it aside.

Academic:
Ricoeur privileges poetic discourse by marking its referent as speculative, not denotive. However, although their reference is speculative, metaphors function cognitively and constitute meanings. . . .[6]

By dissertation standards this pattern is exemplary; it communicates (i.e., doesn't communicate) in a style that suits academic ambitions. Its opacity to all but a few specialized colleagues protects it from barbaric attack. In spite of endless prattle about reforming the scholarly paradigm, this remains the power model. Its severity spills over into other models of academic discourse, including so-called PC (politically correct) expression. *Marginalization; disempowerment;*

unconscionable rapist-aggressiveness; phallocentricity; deprivilegization. By commandeering such language from the behavioral sciences, PC-talk obscures its basis in tolerance and enjoyment of diversity. Attention-getting for a while, the language has sagged under its own weight, stimulated a backlash, lost its gravity in a rash of send-ups (e.g., James Finn Garner's *Politically Correct Bedtime Stories,* Macmillan, 1994, and its sequel).

Commercial:
The New York Times Company is watching the embryonic on-line industries with interest and we are actively reviewing the potential for partnerships and service opportunities. Our continuing emphasis is determining the appropriate strategy for our company so we can identify which opportunity to pursue and when.[7]

A human being would put the thought this way: "I'd love to invest in the on-line industries if I knew which way was up. When I know, I'll take a leap." But a business must sound businesslike in its public statements, which means devoid of fallible human qualities. So the flabby jargon is actually a solid business model for winning consumer faith. "Look how we're making noises," it says. "We obviously know we should be on top of this. Have confidence." The model weakens, however, when any of its verbiage becomes transparent from wear. By now everyone knows that "actively reviewing" means "we've just woken up—what time is it?"

The nonprofit world, once quasi-human in its statements, has gone bottom-line bonkers over the commercial model. Hoping to raise funds for a new branch library, a Chicago community group persuaded a university finance officer to lead the charge. At a neighborhood meeting the officer reported:

We are closing in on the needed revenue sources from government to move forward, and we are close to harnessing the political and governmental leadership that is needed for a new library. . . . The elements are in place.[8]

Unfortunately, not a brick was in place two years later. One would hope for the nonbusiness world to adopt models of forthright expression, distinct from the greasy corporate paradigm; but fat chance. The commercial model is cropping up everywhere, even knocking at the door of literature. A genre called "business fiction" features short plotted narratives and imagined characters who speak in business parables. (Not to be confused with competent business-themed novels.) These moral tales are used in staff training and at conferences. Here's the model: The protagonist, Al, can't sleep. He slips out of bed, away from wife Julie, and stands by the living-room window, where he ponders business problems and strategies back at the plant. Suddenly, Julie is behind him, asking him to come back to bed. He says he's thinking. She asks what's wrong.

> So I tell her: The way our accounting system works, the cost of parts *looks* as though it's gone up because of the additional setups necessitated by the smaller batch sizes.[9]

> **Literary:**
> The turkey stench rose to his nostrils, harsh, penetrating, ammoniac, the smell of the barnyard, manured fields, the dank working mold of the darkest corner of the darkest cellar. . . .
> It was May before the skunk cabbage began to push up through the ooze of the swamps, before the rhubarb reddened the back corner of the garden and the spring peepers finally emerged and began abrading the edges of the night with their lovesick vibrato.
> —T. Coraghessan Boyle, *The Road to Wellville* (Viking, 1993)

Boyle and half the world's writers follow the florid model— textured, lavish, sensuous; a counterpoint to the equally imitated minimalist paradigm. Boyle exploits the sound and rhythm of the language. He pushes old words into new uses, braves the use of little-known words. His ambition is to evoke deep response, engagement, by association; the style suits it.

New Journalistic:
Did I miss something here? The Hutus butcher and maim somewhere between 500,000 and a million Tutsis, hightail it out of Rwanda to Zaire, and the world immediately launches a massive give-as-you've-never-given-before Emergency Relief Effort to save . . . *the Hutus?* Help me understand this.
—Michael O'Donoghue, "Not My Fault," *Spin*, January 1995

The late comedy writer and *Spin* magazine columnist put his own spin on the New Journalism model, that expressively personal approach to newswriting. Here is a distinctively American voice, addressing the grimmest possible topic in the style of stand-up monologue: rhetorical questions, sarcasm, long phrases conscripted into service as modifiers; the style of *Am I crazy? Is it only me?*

Popular:
Tarantino disciples will get a rush from this first full-length docu on the geek-made-good cult helmer. . . .
—Derek Elley, *Variety*[10]

Variety: The International Entertainment Weekly is its own paradigm, a trend-setting promulgator of trendspeak. Its neologisms and playful condensations of language, especially in its headlines ("Oz Goes Boom at B.O.") feed the Hollywood and show-biz models. *Editor & Publisher* columnist Jack Hart called trendspeak "the glib argot of second-rate city magazines and alternative newsweeklies . . . a pastiche of pretentious abstractions, fad words, breezy syntax, overdone alliteration, and sophomoric sociology jargon.''[11] All true, and to be heeded. Trendy or chic words and catchphrases are not for enduring prose. But if the model fits the topic, if it fits your objective, and if you *know* this morning's trend words, then—

NO NEED TO NIX POP P'R'D'GM

11

Other People's Words

True wit is nature to advantage dress'd,
What oft was thought, but ne'er so well express'd.
—Alexander Pope, *Essay on Criticism, II*

*W*hen we encounter exemplary expression—words producing the very effect we long to achieve—we can do two things: (1) emulate it by fashioning our own words after the model, or (2) quote it; that is, borrow someone's else's words to represent our thoughts. Everyone borrows words; some do so more nimbly than others. Expression would be insufferably bleak without the charms and treasures of utterances past. Borrowed words connect us to one another, across periods, across cultures. They affirm the universality of human thought and emotions. And for "one brief shining moment" *(Camelot)* at a time, they make us look good.

"Freedom is like a blanket which, pulled up to the chin, uncovers the feet," I've often said to nods of approval. It so happens that John Updike said these words previously in his novel *The Coup,* but they passed my simple tests of quotability—*I wish I'd said them, and I want to say them.* So into the notebook they went and out they come at appropriate times, usually with credit to Mr. Updike. Not every well-turned phrase can be copied or marked, but those that resonate, those relating to the things I like to talk about, and those not likely to appear in popular quotation books I try to add to my repertoire of expressiveness. The more arcane or private the source, the better; the words will be fresh to my audience. A friend given to quirky outbursts once announced, "I enjoy life through the medium of dread." It made the notebook.

What we think of as familiar or "best-loved" quotes may lack freshness but usually bear repeated hearings. They are best-loved for good reasons, among them:

> **Sound and rhythm:** " 'Twas brillig, and the slithy toves, / Did gyre and gimble in the wabe . . ." (Lewis Carroll)
> **Concise wisdom (economy):** ". . . to thine own self be true . . ." (William Shakespeare)
> **Comfort:** "After all, tomorrow is another day." (Margaret Mitchell)
> **Precision:** "They shall beat their swords into plowshares . . ." (Isaiah 1:18)
> **Humanity:** "Give me your tired, your poor, / Your huddled masses yearning to breathe free." (Emma Lazarus)
> **Wit:** "I never forget a face, but in your case I'll make an exception." (Groucho Marx)
> **Application to one's purpose:** "Rise up, my love, my fair one, and come away." (Song of Solomon 2:10)

Such standbys are durable over the long term but cloying when they come thick and fast. As "brevity is the soul of wit" (Shakespeare), sparsity is the rule of borrowed expressiveness. Expression can drown itself in borrowings. Audiences crave sincerity and spontaneity, both of which are eroded by torrential quotation. Perhaps you know one of those walking compendia of pithy sayings. You fear to mention a word within their hearing. *"Marriage* did you say? 'The only adventure open to the cowardly.' Voltaire. 'A triumph of habit over hate.' Oscar Levant.

'It doesn't go with everything else in the house.' Jean Kerr. . . ." The only greater challenge to listener endurance is a speaker who has passed the night with a toastmaster's quote book:

> You've kindly asked me to review the year on Wall Street. Well, "ask, and it shall be given," but what can I tell you? "You pays your money and you takes your choice." "It was the best of times, it was the worst of times." Were there geniuses? "Genius is one percent inspiration and ninety-nine percent perspiration." Smart money followed the start-ups. "If a man can make a better mousetrap . . . the world will make a beaten path to his door." Were there losers? Hah—"Look how the mighty have fallen in the midst of the battle!" "Beware of false prophets" proved good advice. But "you ain't heard nothin' yet, folks." . . .

True enough, the speaker has delivered nothing. Quotations cannot be used as showy distractions from the emptiness of new messages. A few apt selections break the humdrum of the here-and-now. Too many, and the borrowings become white noise themselves.

In spite of these liabilities, the temptation to seize another's words is overpowering, for rarely has average expression been so impoverished, and never has our inventory of quotations been larger or more accessible. Whatever my thought, an apt quote (or fifty) is at hand.

The world's stock of "noble" words was considerable even before printing, but not so great as to discourage newly quotable expression. "Fame is the perfume of heroic deeds," said Plato, quoting Socrates. That hardly slammed the door on aphorisms about fame. Even after the unsurpassable grace of the Bible, even after the legacies of Shakespeare, Milton, Pope, Samuel Johnson, Coleridge, and Carlyle, to mention just a few much-quoted Brits—there was room for yet more pithy observations on most topics.

Fame is a food that dead men eat—
I have no stomach for such meat.
                    —Austin Dobson

With modern communications and electronic archiving, however, the body of recorded expression grows exponentially, layering the planet with the already-said *about everything*. Most of this expression is retrievable. "Quotable" remarks once gathered as diamonds from select sources are now strip-mined from the entire terrain of expression to feed journalism, scholarship, and the reference industry. For preservation and study this is useful. For choosing one's words it can be overwhelming.

The Oxford English Dictionary, 2d edition (1989, 20 volumes) contains 2,436,600 quotations, and not all of them brief snippets to illustrate usage history. More than 33,000 of the *OED*'s quotations are from Shakespeare alone and some 25,000 are from the Bible. *The Oxford Dictionary of Quotations* offers some 70,000 entries. *The Home Book of Quotations* ("Stevenson") puts about 50,000 on the table; the 1992 *Familiar Quotations* ("Bartlett's," which first appeared in 1855) runs to almost 800 pages of judiciously selected quotations. These sources overlap somewhat, but there are hundreds of collections of English quotations, proverbs, epigrams, meditations, slogans, mottoes, maxims, one-liners, and so on, not to mention the equivalents in other major languages.

Practically every cogent sound bite from the recent or distant past is vacuumed into huge general collections or gathered in specialized collections under every imaginable topic or popular category: best quotes, unkind quotes, love quotes, war quotes, women's quotes, black quotes, Yiddish quotes, gay quotes, garden quotes. Or fighting words, inspirational words, last words, and so on. All this ready-made expression, as eager to jump into my prose as dust onto my monitor! Whatever I mean to say, someone always seems to have said it more eloquently, more pointedly, more vigorously. Even Samuel Clemens, Jr., one of the most quoted of all Americans, envied the virgin territory of the earliest wordsmith, Adam: "When he said a good thing, he knew nobody had said it before."

Power Quoting

Here is the most intimidating development of all: *Now, in an electronic instant, I can retrieve quotations applying to any imaginable topic.* Reference publishers are issuing or licensing massive collections of quotes on electronic databases. Packaged for the desktop computer, these collections put the cream of the world's concise expression on a few discs the size of tea saucers. Boot up, and you are master of a court of wits numbering in the thousands. "I wish to speak of 'roses' and 'love'!" you decree, and—*click*—scores of offerings parade before your eyes to suit every desired nuance.

Some products at this writing: *The Oxford Dictionary of Quotations and Modern Quotations* squeezes some 22,500 quotations and a powerful searching program on three-and-a-half-inch diskettes. A few mouse clicks and the chosen quote is in your text. (The complete *OED*, 2d ed., is also available in electronic form.) With a more American slant, *The Columbia Electronic Dictionary of Quotations* brings 18,000 entries to the fingertip. Should your fingertip lack even the first notion of what subject it craves, click on a "lightbulb" icon: A random quotation will appear at your service. A higher-end tool meant to be used in libraries is *Gale's Quotations,* containing 117,000 quotations that can be dragged into your text. All these collections draw heavily on poetry, owing to its compressed and lyrical nature. *Poem Finder,* a compact-disc product, indexes key words, subjects, and more in a database of *400,000* poems. Stick in your thumb and pull out a plum.

Public and Private Quoting

In view of such tempting abundance, Joseph Roux's admonition is truer than ever: "A fine quotation is a diamond on the finger of a man of wit, and a pebble in the hand of a fool." Using quotes in public expression calls for the same discrimination and agonizing over effect that goes into choosing one's own words. Just sorting through the universe of possibilities is challenge enough, but once you present someone else's expression as part of yours, you are judged by it. Was the quotation to the point? Did it respect or at least acknowledge the audience's intelligence and tastes? Was it fresh or presented in a fresh context? *Was it quoted accurately?* To most modern audiences, a quote such as "Hell hath no fury like a woman scorned" may miss on all four counts. ("Heaven has no rage like love to hatred turned/Nor hell a fury like a woman scorned." —William Congreve, *The Mourning Bride.*)

You might be further judged on how you have misunderstood a quote or twisted it to your own purposes. Many thousands of popular phrases have strayed from the source quotation, for better or worse. "He who hesitates is lost" is said to be a distortion of Joseph Addison's "The woman that deliberates is lost" *(Cato)* and probably for the better. Sometimes a shortening known as a "tag" is a practical variant. "There's a method to his madness" derives from "Though this be madness, yet there is method in't" *(Hamlet).* If time allows, all quotations should be checked, but most audiences are forgiving (or unaware) of minor misquotation, especially in speech. Now and then I would hear convention speakers say "growed like Topsy" in this sense: "Well, interest rates plunged, and stocks just growed like Topsy!" Ignorant of the source, I finally checked to see who this ballooning Topsy might be. The quote is from Harriet Beecher Stowe's *Uncle Tom's Cabin* and goes like this:

[Aunt Ophelia] "Do you know who made you?"
[Topsy, the slave girl] "Nobody, as I knows on," said the
child with a short laugh. "I 'spect I grow'd."

A more accurate use: "We don't know why, but we 'spect that,
like Topsy, stocks just . . . grow'd."

In public speaking or writing, repeating the words of others
is an art achieved with some anxiety. The joys of private quotation are another matter. Reading and repeating a variety of
quotes to oneself is potent medicine that goes down pleasantly.
What quicker way to get the tongue around new and refreshing patterns? What better exercise for muscling thoughts into
words? Writing down stimulating quotes, whether from published collections or your own readings, will help invigorate
your way of speaking even if you don't use the quotations publicly.

We expand our language capacity with quotes, including
those from periods whose vocabulary and syntax seem quaint.
Chaucer's "It is nought good a sleyping hound to wake" offers
more to chew on than the prosaic "Let sleeping dogs lie."
Because we find charm and refreshment in archaic- and poetic-
sounding word order, we often favor antiqued translations. We
prefer "one swallow does not a summer make" to ". . . does
not make a summer," although the Greek and Spanish sources
could be translated either way.

The best quotations offer more than a pretty string of words.
They encapsulate general wisdom and illuminate our thinking.
Longer quotes—those more than a few sentences—may be
what Winston Churchill had in mind when he said, "It is a
good thing for an uneducated man to read books of quotations." It doesn't hurt educated men and all women, either.

Let Sleyping Catchphrases Lie

What does hurt is repeating other people's pat (or pet) phrases only to feel them dropping dead from your lips. Maybe they had more pop when you heard them, freshly plucked from a commercial or comedy sketch. Maybe certain other people had a way of putting them over. In casual use you might squeeze one more response from "reality check," "game plan" or "out of control." But by the time you get them into a speech or article, they have all the force of a proverb painted on shellacked wood: Vee grow too soon oldt und too late schmart, ya?

Car dealers speak of "previously owned" autos these days instead of "used" cars. "Previously owned" suggests premium quality well preserved. "Used" connotes beat up, on its last legs. Other people's words can be viewed in such terms. Quotes such as Marshall McLuhan's "The medium is the message" or Andy Warhol's "In the future everybody will be world-famous for fifteen minutes" are rent-a-wrecks. They have 200,000 miles on them and have blown their rods. Previously owned words such as these of Roman lexicographer Festus keep purring away:

> We live in deeds, not years; in thoughts, not breaths; in feelings, not in figures on a dial. . . . He most lives who thinks most, feels the noblest, acts the best.

Rules of Attribution and General Use

We quote not only to reinforce and embellish our messages, but to deviate from predictable expression. Deviousness taxes our inventiveness to the limit, so we get help: Here and there we borrow deviant expression from others. In doing so we still serve our audiences by stimulating them, assuming they have not been overexposed to the borrowing. Describing some classically awful film, for example, I might use the oxymoron "treasurably bad," which I spotted in a *New York Times* review by John Rockwell. But what about attribution? Do I credit Rockwell, respecting the creativity he put into that phrase?

In formal quotation of any length, we credit the source. In casual use of others' expression, we give credit if we know the source and if our audience is likely to care. Writing for publication or speaking publicly, I would certainly give Rockwell his due, even for two words; I would do the same in an academic paper. Yakking with friends, I might slip the phrase in and skip any pedantic-sounding attribution. If they remark on it, I will confess the borrowing.

We all repeat those phrases that seem to be of general ownership, often without knowing the source. But of course we stop short of two sins. Briefly described they are:

Copyright infringement: Illegal use of published or unpublished writing (words in tangible form) that is protected under copyright. From the time of its creation, most original writing is now protected for the lifetime of the author plus fifty years. (Earlier legislation allowed for different terms, so that most material older than seventy-five years is in the public domain, along with U.S. government publications.) Copyright law, however, allows for limited "fair use" of protected material for such purposes as criticism, commentary, and news reporting. Key factors in judging fair use are: How commercial is the use? How much of the work's "essence" is borrowed? What proportion of the full work is used? How does the borrowing affect the market for the original? Practice in the publishing industry indicates that borrowing up to three hundred words of an average book-length (prose) work is fair use for criticism, commentary, or news, provided those words are not of some extraordinary value in the original (for example, the ending of a mystery thriller). But beware unauthorized use of even a single line of protected poetry or song, and limit borrowings from short prose works to some fifty words or five percent, whichever is less. Like all borrowed material, fair-use items should be credited. Beyond fair use, the copyright owner's permission is required, and permission often comes with a fee.

Plagiarism: Presenting *as your own* a cluster of words you know to be someone else's. In writing that is not to be published, such as a course paper, plagiarism is an ethical problem undone by citations that credit the source. In works for publication or public performance, plagiarizing copyrighted material is both unethical and illegal, with serious penalties. Representing even uncopyrighted material as your own work is just plain pathetic.

· · ·

So much for the legal/ethical rules. To help cap our general discussion, here are seven rules of thumb (six of them borrowed) on borrowing other people's words:

1. If you've heard it twice in the last year, don't use it. That should take care of "May the wind always be at your back" and sayings like it.

   (Four rules from librarian and educator Charles Curran[1]:)
2. Repeat a platitude, expect an attitude.
3. Declare a dictum, reside in hickdom.
4. Mouth a cliché, you're passé.
5. Proverb, schmahverb.
6. "Everything has already been said but, since no one pays attention, it has to be repeated each morning." (attributed to Marcel Proust by Camilo José Cela)
7. "I hate quotations. Tell me what you know." (Ralph Waldo Emerson)

12

Infusions for
Tired Vocabularies

*H*ow we love acquiring words, words that suit us, *trophy* words that make us feel like winners. At first we can't love them enough. See how the manager adores her *right sizing* and *reengineering*, the poet his *chanfron etched with bands of tansies, knuckled anarchy of art.*[1] But we are fickle lovers. Soon we tire of the familiar and pursue what philanderers call the taste of *strange*, of something not yet savored. If there is maleness to this metaphor, so it goes, for we have our fling with new words only to abandon them when they become common property, packraped by the masses and the media. Someday in a home for aged expression, *parenting, empowerment, couch potato,* and their cronies will tell how once they were loved to distraction.

Why do humans crave novelty in language? Blame the survival instinct: Fresh stimuli fire up our neurons, keeping us on the *qui vive* for danger and opportunity. But enough anthroposemiotic musing! The observable fact is that we seek newness in expression: new names for yet-unnamed objects and phenomena and new ways to talk about old things. We want fresher words for old meanings, new combinations that add precision, new words that surprise us in pleasing ways. We want old words bent and stretched into clever new uses.

As a nation we consume novel wordage as ravenously as we guzzle our resources. In quieter times a new locution might have enjoyed a few leisurely hours before being sucked into the maw of public expression. Today the demands of incessant and instantaneous global communications allow no such respite. Like vampires, the more we slake our thirst, the more we must stalk the alleys of language for *neologisms*—new words, or new uses of old ones.

Knowing the dynamics of new-word formation—how the language keeps growing—gives one a *leg up* in the hunt for novel expression. A linguistics course is not required, just a masterly introduction to neologisms such as appears in *Fifty Years Among the New Words: A Dictionary of Neologisms, 1941–1991*, edited by John Alego (Cambridge University Press, 1991). Covering *blitz* (1940), *boy toy* (1990), and some four thousand other terms, the book reprints half a century's worth of new-word sightings and commentary from "Among the New Words," a column in the journal *American Speech*.[2] The following little primer draws from Alego's lengthy introduction and numerous other sources.[3]

Elements of New-Word Formations

• In general, neologisms are terms and meanings that have come into the common or working vocabulary of English speakers but are not yet in standard reference works. A neologism can be a single word *(guesstimate)*, a compound *(white flight)*, or an idiomatic phrase *(fun and games)*. Alego calls these words and combinations "forms."

• Many new forms proliferate and die quickly as "nonce" words. For almost every public scandal since Watergate, for example, someone has created a nonce word ending in *-gate*. Nonce words may not make it to the dictionaries, but they exemplify "a spirit of play that has as much claim to being a central function of language as any of the more sober purposes usually set forth as humanity's reason for talking." (Alego)

- Some major providers of new forms: science and technology, including medicine; the military; entertainment; ethnic, regional, student, and gay subcultures; political and sports journalism; food and drink; advertising.
- How does a language get its new forms? Here are six basic etymological sources for English neologisms:

Creating: Complete new inventions—not formed from existing words. *Boondoggle.* Rare, except for new words that imitate sounds *(bleep, chugalug, burp).* A "coinage," by the way, is not necessarily an invention in this pure sense; it refers to a deliberately created form, usually attributed to an individual. George Orwell's *newspeak* and *doublethink* are coinages created by the process of "combining" existing words (see below).

Borrowing: (1) Simple "loanwords" adopted from other languages directly into English with no changes or only minor ones for pronunciation *(aprés-ski* from French, *flack* from German, *apartheid* from Afrikaans); (2) adapted or remodeled loanwords *(cybernetics* from the Greek *kybernetes);* (3) loan translations, or foreign terms shoehorned into existing English words *(found object* from *objet trouvé).*

Combining: Probably the most fecund of all sources. Existing words or word parts (morphemes) are combined into new forms *(granny-bashing, reality check, dullsville).* The elements to be combined include whole words, base parts, and affixes (prefixes, infixes, and suffixes). New or revived affixes such as *green-, eco-, mega-,* or *-nik* set off swarms of neologisms. Rhyme, alliteration, and vowel repetition also inspire new combinations *(brain drain, shock jock, roid rage, date rape).* Note that combining often links incongruous elements to create tension or comedy. Take the suffix *-ectomy,* for example, and try preceding it not with body organs but with things or people you'd like to see removed from your life: "What this country needs is an immediate_____-ectomy!"

Shortening: Words are constantly clipped head, tail, or within to form new variations *(dis* from disrespect; *indie* from independent producer; *do* from hairdo). Poet Robert Pinsky declared he was "not overwhelmed" by sudden attention, just *whelmed*—a type of shortening called "back-formation" in that the word goes "back" to a bogus original form. The verb *to lech* is back-formed from "lecher" and "lechery." Other shortenings include "initialisms" *(V.I.P.)* and "acronyms" *(AIDS).*

Blending: A simultaneous combining and shortening *(fanzine,* from "fan" plus "magazine"). Two or more forms are joined, but at least part of one is omitted. *Slumlord* omits the "land" of "landlord." *Infotainment* clips both "mation" and "enter" from the source words. A sly blending of commonly shared syllables or sounds makes for words like *affluenza, rockumentary, Reaganomics, quack-upuncture, threepeat.* Blending accounts for only some five to ten percent of new forms, but many of the most endearing ones. Dick Thurner, a *wordaholic* (my term, I think) who collects blendings, notes that they are also called portmanteaus, centaur words, amalgams, mongrel words, brunch words, fusions, and telescope words, in case anyone asks.

Shifting: Like most of the universe, words won't stay put. They shift into: new meanings *(streak,* to dash naked in public); new grammatical functions *(out,* v., to reveal one's homosexuality); new spellings *(Amerika, thang, gangsta rap),* and so on. **Eponymic naming,** or turning names of people into nouns, modifiers, and verbs, might be seen as a special kind of shifting. The eponymic device is used widely, from science *(Gooch crucible)* to popular culture. "The June bug *Jackson Pollocked* my windshield . . ." begins an ad for radio shows with "substance."

How Shifting Impacts Bums

Many people are flustered by unregulated changes to the existing order, and shifting is just such a change. *Impact* was basically a noun whose only verbal function had to do with meteors hitting planets. When writers started downshifting the verb into a mere substitute for "affect," several language guardians considered the planet doomed—and still do. But shifting or extending the functions of a word *(enallage)* is as old as language and figurative speech. English easily accommodates such shifting; American English thrives on it. Although some derivatives—for example, those from Greek or Latin—resist change of function, it seems that once a word makes its way to America, it acts like an American; i.e., it aspires to be all that it can be:

Deriving from the German *bummler,* or drunken loafer, *bum* showed up in Oregon in 1855 as a noun. Now a bum (noun) with a bum (adjective) leg can bum (verb) a ride to Arizona and bum-trip (adverb-like) on peyote. Recently the adjective *dumb,* as in stupid, made a smooth transition to verb and gerund, partly because intellectuals found it useful: "They are trying to *dumb down* the curriculum"; "The *dumbing* of America." And on March 13, 1995, the word became a noun in an article by Rich Cohen entitled "The Dawn of Dumb" *(The New York Times,* op-ed page). Remarking on "the new craze for stupidity," Cohen observed: "Dumb is modern in a way the French will never understand."

Common Sources of the Uncommon

Neologisms are but one means of achieving novelty, of deviating from the ordinary. Another way is to find existing but uncommon words and word meanings that hit home or simply delight. Americans tend to communicate within a minuscule vocabulary, yet they can recognize or at least appreciate a much greater range of words. The stage is set, then, for stimulating the average audience with something from this broader range. But exactly what? Where are the words found?

Two types of sources provide such infusions: sources that many share but few exploit, such as dictionaries; and sources encountered on one's own, such as readings, specialized word lists, expressive people. If a new term is juicy enough, use it, without worrying unduly if it can be understood. Sound alone can stimulate, and meanings can be surmised from context or looked up later. I throw around the term *superluminal quantum interconnectedness* as a state of being I hope to achieve one day. So what if only two physicists on earth know what it means?

Travels in Dictionaries. Rarely heard terms can be as fresh as neologisms—and as stimulating, provided their meanings are suggested in some painless manner. To most audiences the bulk of words even in abridged dictionaries would be fresh, not to mention the riches of the queenly lexicons. Thus an aspiring wordmeister's first thought might be to "study" the nearest unabridged Webster's. The usual resolve is to start approximately at *aalii* and proceed systematically toward *Zyryan.* People who set out to study whole dictionaries, however, usually despair somewhere around *axolotl,* one salamander too many to pack in one's vocabulary.

Rambling in a dictionary is another matter. Here one dodges the crowds to sojourn with forgotten acquaintances and inviting strangers. For example, my opening one unabridged dictionary[4] to a random page yielded these companionable terms among others (definitions not verbatim, examples my own):

jejune (ji joon) *adj.* A novel (and sometimes mockingly pretentious) synonym for "dull," "insipid," "uninformed," or "immature," "juvenile." E.g., Americans appear jejune among the more sophisticated Europeans.

jen (zhun) *n.* In Chinese philosophy, a compassionate love for humanity or for the world as a whole. E.g., Though Americans may appear jejune, they have a compensating jen.

jeremiad (jer ə miəd) *n.* A prolonged lamentation or mournful complaint, the sort we inflict on listeners after a day at the office. E.g., His nightly jeremiads wore her down.

jessant (jes ənt) *adj.* Shooting up, as a plant (not as a junkie), or coming forth, issuant. The rarity of "jessant" outside Heraldic use, along with its energetic meaning and pleasant sound, make it a good candidate for adaptation. E.g., Her adolescence was brief, jessant; overnight she seemed to pass from child into woman.

Terms gathered in such ambles may be saved in notebooks or not, for once the ambler has discovered the profusion of life under every few letters of the alphabet, there is no escape from word addiction. Feeding that addiction, in good dictionaries, are word derivations, or *etymologies,* which are no less fascinating for their being theoretical in many cases. What, for example, is the derivation of *jerk* as a verb meaning to pull, twist, move with a sudden, arrested motion? Our dictionary theorizes that an old shoemaker's term—*yerk,* to draw stitches tight and thus make the shoe ready to wear—might have been the link between the Old English *gearcian,* to make ready, and our modern *jerk.* If this tidbit occupies your thoughts the next time a slugger *jerks* one out of the ballpark, you may qualify as a bona fide word nut.

Etymologies are only one of many dictionary pleasures; others include usage notes and examples; obsolete words that beg for revival *(bedswerver,* an unfaithful spouse); the often-astounding earliest appearances of words *(duds* as clothing, A.D. 1275; *jargon,* A.D. 1300); synonyms, antonyms (opposites); pronunciation notes; regionalisms (*cooter,* a turtle in the South); and style labels ("offensive," "literary," "baby talk," etc.). Not all such features yield expressive new words, but in deepening one's addiction, they lead to other supply sources, such as thematic word collections, thesauruses, and specialized glossaries.

Collecting from Collections. To compile a typical word collection, an author pores through a general dictionary for terms that fit a chosen theme, such as "lost words," or "power words," or "words on words." *The New York Times Everyday Reader's Dictionary of Misunderstood, Misused, and Mispronounced Words* (Times Books) is a personalized collection by lexicographer Laurence Urdang. Collectors supplement the dictionary terms with words gathered from readings, historical research, and spoken expression in various subcultures. They rummage for other odds and ends such as record-setting words: Chargoggagoggmanchauggagoggchaubunagungamaugg is a lake in Massachusetts and the longest U.S. place name. Don't try to say it.

Urdang's collection is billed as "a dictionary minus the mundane," favoring the oddball, the fancy, and the sesquipedalian (many-syllabic). Most of it is for the fun of browsing, yet here and there a term both novel and manageable turns up to freshen ordinary vocabularies. *Limen* (līmən), for example, means psychological threshold, or the point at which a stimulus reaches sufficient intensity to produce a perceptible effect. "Your flirtations slide beneath my limen of interest." Another ambitious collection (the *Random House Dictionary for Writers and Readers,* by David Grambs) is hyped on its cover as "more than 2,000 whimsical, literary, outrageous, picturesque, provocative, witty, impertinent, and even practical words on language." Here, among such terms as *florilegium* (an anthology) and *perpilocutionist* (hypocrite), are the little-heard *gnomic* (pithily expressive of wise truths), the forgotten *framis* (high-level, comical double-talk), and other usable infusions. "Just spew a lot of framis and pause; they'll think you're as gnomic as Voltaire.''

As diverting as they may be, most word collections fail to deliver enough practical words to justify serious A-to-Z study. (Practical words abound in so-called vocabulary builders, but such thirty-day wonders offer little to excite the word enthusiast.) To distinguish their lists, word collectors seize exotic terms that cry out for cautionary advice on usage, but such caution is rarely given. *Eleemosynary* (charitable) is the sort of term found in ''word-lovers'' collections with no tips on when to trot it out. Recently, when the new conglomerate ruler of an old publishing house stated, ''We're obviously not an eleemosynary institution and we want to make money,''[5] it seemed merely show-offish.

Roget's Treasury. *Eleemosynary* might also have been plucked too quickly from a thesaurus, an indispensable word-finding tool that teems with possibilities for novel expression. A true thesaurus organizes terms by meaning, rather than alphabetically. It groups those that are similar in intent and provides cross-references to related terms. Usually at least one term in a group is the *perfect*—or should we say *ideal, impeccable, right as rain, consummate, unsurpassable, apt, recherché, felicitous?*—choice for a given situation; but if the choice isn't obvious, the most promising words must be further explored in dictionaries or usage guides. Skipping this extra step often leads to bungled expression. *Recherché* prose, for example, can mean painstakingly chosen, rare, uncommon, arcane, obscure, or precious and pretentious prose—quite a range. Bungling is part of learning, however, and a thesaurus is an incomparable starting place in the search for alternative and exact words.

The word *thesaurus* itself was well chosen when a British publisher issued the first *Roget's Thesaurus of English Words and Phrases* in 1852; it derives from the Greek *thesauros,* or treasure house—thus, a treasure house of words. Peter Mark Roget

(1779–1869) completed this work only after a vigorous career as a physician, mathematician, scientist, and scholar.[6] His was the sort of wide-ranging intelligence that could solve London's water filtration problem, invent the log-log scale used on slide rules, and classify an enormous collection of words according to the *ideas* they express.

Roget's classified thesaurus is the genuine article and the most stimulating type of word-finder. Entering it is like driving into a well-marked landscape of busy word-villages, each specializing in a particular concept, each eager to point to concepts down the road. I arrive in *Dimness* and after a feast of dimness terms I am told, "Oh, you must visit *Greyness!* You'll love it in *Darkness,* or *Half-Light, Glimmer, Shadowy,* and *Blur.* And when you're tired of dimness country, try *Light!*" (Each concept is bordered by its opposite.) Next to the open country of a thesaurus, a mere list of synonyms seems claustrophobic.

Below, the object is to improve on the word *great* in uses such as "The film was great." It was great how? Start in the left-hand column.

Synonym Lists

(1) A list of pre-chosen alternatives are given under *great* in synonym dictionaries, alphabetical "thesauruses," and computer "thesauruses" (which are essentially lists of synonyms and antonyms). One looks up *great* and finds varied but nondistinguishing options such as these:

Magnificent, outstanding, distinguished, superb, excellent, exceptional, superior,

Thesaurus

(1) Under *great* in the index to *Roget's Thesaurus* are listed fourteen broad meanings of the word, among them: superior, powerful, influential, important, excellent, super. (2) From these, one chooses a likely direction. Each choice leads to hundreds of words and concepts related to that particular sense of *great.* For example, *important* leads to a page of terms gathered under *impor-*

splendid, majestic, grand, fine, prime, sovereign, first-class, top-flight.

(2) Looking up synonyms for some of these options yields such additional choices as these:

surpassing, noble, matchless, incomparable, marvelous, wonderful, astonishing, amazing, exemplary, laudable, extraordinary, glorious, striking, choice, fabulous, fantastic, spectacular, remarkable.

These are serviceable substitutes for *great,* varying in emphasis. Any more-imaginative directions, however, must be prompted by the searcher's own conceptual ingenuity. Now read the adjacent column.

tance. Here one finds dozens of vivid alternatives to *great* in this particular sense, along with pointers to related meanings that will stretch the concept. A sampling:

weighty, world-shattering, momentous, pivotal, vital, signal, bedrock, commanding, imposing, stirring, formidable, impressive, breathtaking, earth-shaking, epoch-making, telling, trenchant.

Following just one pointer, to *impressive* (classified under terms of *excitation*), opens up another conceptual domain, with such options to *great* as *feverish, inspired, rousing, gripping,* and *agitating.*

Special Word Sources

A special source is one *not* designed as a general word reference. Your own incidental readings—books, articles, news reports—are special sources because not everyone else is reading them to find new expression. When you do so, you are likely to capture terms that will be fresh to your next audiences.

While writing this chapter I happened to be reading a film review by Anthony Lane, admiring his catch of lively words in the overfished waters of criticism. Here are some of the fresh terms, revivals, new uses, and novel combinations that thrashed like silvery pike in a bucket: *limpet; footloose and wacky; petty-picaresque; Expressionist jag; riposte; slushy kiss; mid-coital yelp; fortissimo conclusion; flash of loopiness; grunge pose; ridges of threat; dopey unforgettable dawn; as surely as John Cheever colonized the cocktail hour.*[7] In a few months I won't remember which film was being reviewed *(Before Sunrise,* a romance that begins on a European train), but I will salt away some of that language. A term not in my active vocabulary, for example, was *limpet,* a conical marine creature that clings to rocks, and thus a fine metaphor for clinginess or tenacity. "Hang in there like a limpet," is how Lane used it, and as far as I know, the image has not been overdone.

The following is a small sampling of terms, some of them neologisms, that I have encountered in recent and diverse readings (and listenings) and added to my inventory of infusions. Help yourself to anything you like. (Definitions and usage examples here are minimal and more or less of my own fashioning.)

barmy, *adj.* Frothy, after the barm or froth in beer-making; not very substantial. E.g., You've found a barmy way to answer the question.

hoover, *v., tr.* To suck in, as does a Hoover vacuum cleaner. E.g., We have black holes hoovering half the universe.

brio, *n.* Upbeat energy, vigor. **Schadenfreude,** *n.* Pleasure or satisfaction at someone's misfortune. E.g., Such brio at his funeral hinted at schadenfreude.

manueline, *n., adj.* An ornate, exuberant style of Portuguese architecture (1490–) with intricately intertwined motifs from exploration and astronomy. Thus, a special worldly complexity. E.g., her manueline soul.

hyaline, *adj.* Glassy and transparent or translucent. E.g., a face in the hyaline shallows of the pond.

himbo, *n.* A male bimbo, good-looking and unintelligent.

morbidezza, *n.* (Italian). A resilient softness, as of fresh bread.

E.g., He felt the warmth of her cheeks and their morbidezza, forbidden to him.

tenebrous, *adj.* Dark, gloomy, obscure. E.g., another day in these tenebrous wastelands.

raffish, *adj.* Two conflicting meanings: disreputable in a naughty, unconventional, engaging way—"Take off that wig, you raffish fool!"—or in a vulgar, tawdry, *churlish* (rude, boorish) way.

sui generis, *adj.* (Latin). One of a kind, unique. E.g., a sui generis beauty if I ever saw one.

fustian, *n., adj.* A stout cloth; turgid, inflated language in speaking or writing. E.g., Lincoln's early speeches were in the fustian of his time.

gravitas, *n.* A solemn bearing; serious-mindedness. E.g., I appreciate your concern, but please—spare me the gravitas.

frisson, *n.* (French). A sudden surge or shudder of emotion. E.g., Lying gave him a little frisson of rebellion.

cosmic gloaming, *n.* The cosmic twilight, or end of the world. E.g., Don't jabber till the cosmic gloaming; just yes or no.

low-center-of-gravity guy, *n.* A wide, heavy male, as a football lineman. E.g., I don't argue with low-center-of-gravity guys.

sokaiya, *n.* (Japanese). Gangs of Japanese toughs who threaten to disrupt business meetings if not paid off. E.g., When the Republicans balked, the President did everything but call in the sokaiya.

mephitis, *n.* A hideous stench, usually from below. E.g., The mephitis rising from the dungeon told me of horrors yet to come.

nizhoni, *n.* (Navajo). "Walking in beauty," or relating harmoniously to one's environment. E.g., Just give me the tour, pal, I don't need to reach nizhoni.

yoik, *n., v.* (Sami). Glottal, yelping, singsong chants of the

Lapps (Samis), once religious, now secularized. E.g., One off-color remark and the students are yoiking for my resignation!

Special word sources include the myriad lists and dictionaries produced for particular subject fields or interests. (See also next chapter and Resources.) Here one finds not only curious names of things in each specialty, but fresh-sounding terms to adapt to one's own applications. From science terminology alone, humanists can borrow enough language to replace every tired metaphor in print. If scientists can crib *quark* from James Joyce, humanists can appropriate *podzol, apogee, chiasma, neap tides,* and *nictitating membrane* from the nearest science dictionary. Be warned, however, that once humanists use a science word, its *half-life* can be brief indeed. For scientists a word simply designates something for all time; humanists exhaust words by burdening them with the need to stimulate, stretching them into new meanings until they wear thin. In 1994 someone used *tsunami* (an enormous wave produced by a seaquake or undersea volcanic eruption) as an apt metaphor for the Republican victory at the polls; it was so used fourteen times in *The New York Times* within a month.

But no matter; the well of science terminology is bottomless. Science produces most of the new words in English, and only a fraction appear in the general dictionaries. Names of more than 750,000 insect species alone are standing by for humanist use. Why should entomologists such as Howard Ensign Evans have all the fun writing about *silver-washed fritillaries, firebrats, symphilids,* and *screwworms?* There are images here, many of them high-spirited and whimsical. *Purple-headed sneezeweed, tufted titmouse,* and *stinkhorn fungus* are gifts from the common-name lexicon of biology. If I needed a fresh profanity, the word *bleb* would be my candidate. "Those killers aren't humans—they're *blebs!*" What is a bleb? Start with the agent of dreaded Lyme disease, a bacterial spirochete called *Borrelia burgdorferi.* When the spirochete grows, it discards material from its outer membrane—material that floats in the blood and cerebrospinal fluid to decoy the immune system and even cause it to attack the host. These insidious bacterial discards are called—what else?—blebs.

Common names aside, science nomenclature brings with it the resonance of classical Greek and Latin, stately melody in our humdrum lives and expression. The "binomial" scheme by which Carolus Linnaeus named the plant and animal kingdoms combines a generic name (Latin, Latinized Greek, or Greek construct) with a unique species name (usually Latin or Latinized). *Gromphadorhina portentosa* is the grand name for cockroach. To our deprived ears, the euphony of Greek *(polyembryony)* or Latin alone is often like a doctor's prescription. Try this: The next time headache strikes deep at the base of the skull, leaving you blocked, cotton-headed, and bereft of invention, repeat this mantra:

> *Medulla oblongata, medulla oblongata,*
> *corpus callosum, medulla oblongata . . .*

Homespun or Whim-Wham?

How does word infusion relate to your own expression? Should you be spinning out neologisms? Raiding the specialized vocabularies? Shifting every other word to its limits? That depends. Writers for such majestically hip magazines as *Wired* and *Spin* shoot the works, assuring readers of yet one more excursion beyond the curve. In a current issue of *Spin* I find a smorgasbord of new terms (new to me as I read them), including: *undie-rock, pantyhose-head, spritzes* (for "says"), *retro glam, shempdom, hook-savvy, post-thriftstore-apocalypse, woozed-out,* and *jungle-ambient.* For audiences attuned to the frenetic stimulation of rock music or computer hacking, prose has to go *balls to the wall* to compete. For other, less rush-dependent audiences, neologisms are most effective when spare and selective, as with any element that calls attention to itself. The most enduring attention falls upon expressiveness as a whole, upon patterns seamlessly woven, with just enough *whim-wham* to catch the eye.

13

Specialized Words:
Stimulation
for Every Occasion

*S*timulation is what we want in expression. Stimulation! Not as in phone sex, perhaps, though such *talking personals* deserve study elsewhere. Here we mean "stimulation" in a less steamy sense (sorry, students), the way it came into English from Latin in the sixteenth century.

Stimulare and related Latin words mean to *prick, goad, spur, urge.* Often we feel lucky just to catch a listener's attention, but life demands more of expression. Countless occasions call for stimulating language—words to stimulate the listener to *do* something, and not just comprehend or appreciate a thought. Words must *prick* an audience into laughing at your act. *Goad* them into eating your expensive cuisine. *Spur* them to fight for your side. *Urge* them to buy a luxury item.

In most instances stimulation can be achieved with a general vocabulary if the principles of forceful expression—discussed earlier—are applied. English, however, has branched into thousands of specialized vocabularies and patterns to fit particular occasions and purposes. Sailing. Stock investment. Pig farming. Politics. All have their inside jargon—in effect, their codes. While some codes simply communicate ideas, others stimulate people to behave or react in certain ways: If I shout *fore!* on the golf links, you are stimulated to duck my usual slice onto the wrong fairway. Not only do specialized words contribute to stimulation within the specialty, but often they have a vitality that can be borrowed for general use. "They've just put Plotnik in charge of operations. *Fore!*"

Specialized English may account for half the language; it increases as fast as new fields and interests develop, and it moves in and out of Standard English with mixed effects. It can be as codified as the name of an ice-skating move—the *triple lutz-double toe loop combination*—or as subtle and organic as the language of courtship or of humor. It may distinguish itself by words—*cowabunga!* (from surfer lingo)—or by patterns. Flight attendants employ a distinctively hospitable yet hostile pattern, a voice of paternal authority that could have been scripted by Freud. *Once again—the captain has asked that all passengers remain seated until the aircraft has come to a complete halt at the landing gate! [Your father has asked that you stay on the toilet until you make!]*

Like hobbyists who find uses for scrap, word people love to rummage through specialized expression. They admire its particularity of purpose. They jump on opportunities to adapt it, if only for laughs. In your search for stimulating language, never snub a specialized glossary that comes your way, however aberrant or alien. Below we rummage through just a few choice areas.

And How Is That Prepared?

A trendy Los Angeles restaurant and another in Miami were kind enough to let me take their menus as souvenirs. Back home I could study the patterns used to stimulate my appetite and ravage my Visa account. Why had I paid $47.50 for a dish of lubricated veggies? Because *haute cuisine* patterns swept me in: *roasted ratatouille terrine with roasted garlic, garlic flowers and virgin olive oil, Napoleon of dehydrated curly cabbage with autumn forest mushrooms, and tricolored Brunoise Risotto of wild rice with roasted nuts.* A separate dessert menu offered pure sensuous poetry, including *gateau of warm chocolate decadence with orange, tangerine sorbet,* and *study of an apple, exposed at its best.*

In Miami I agonized between ordering a chunk of root— *yucca-stuffed picadillo of wild mushrooms, on a bed of sautéed spinach with beet and carrot vinaigrette*—or a piece of rear appendage: *braised oxtail in a fiery La Mancha red wine sauce, dotted with Scotch bonnet pepper sauce, with a plaintain ginger flan and lily rice.* Dessert was a pile of wet cake . . . *soaked in three milks, layered with Kahlua mousse, covered with chocolate meringue and served with chocolate sherbet.*

In dining parlance the particular names of many foods and exotic brands are stimulating enough, but notice all the verb forms to indicate *fussing* on your behalf. In Miami your food was *dressed, tossed, brushed, dusted, saffron-scented, citrus-planked,* and *pan-seared,* among other considerate acts. Coddled diners now question the preparation of every comestible from mashed potatoes up, as well as the prior lifestyle of dead meat. "Was it *free range?*"

Wine connoisseurs used to be a select group sharing a specialized code, but now such terms as *body, bouquet, robust,* and *supple* stimulate millions of occasional tasters. *Oenologists,* or wine experts, merit our attention because they seek standardized words for something as subjective as thoughts; namely, taste perceptions. Once standardized, the words can trigger appropriate wine-purchasing behavior among the cognoscenti. If I tell you a wine is *chewy, developed,* or *nervous,* order a case. *Buttery* or *mousy,* take a pass. In building a common language, says Andrew Sharp in his elegant *Winetaster's Secrets,* "we've come a very long way. Our vinuous vocabulary today consists of about one thousand, reasonably understood words. A few hundred years ago it was less than a hundred."[1] *Pétillant* (light bubbliness) and *quaffable* (inviting and easy to swallow) are two of many terms worth borrowing from Sharp's glossary.

From Phreaking to Clustergeeking

As *ullage* (space between cork and wine) is to oenologists, *shovelware* (fill for leftover space on a CD-ROM) is to computer hackers, who are one of the most prolific and conflicted generators of new expression. Within the computer subculture, would-be hackers *(wanna-bes)* who overuse hacker vocabulary only condemn themselves to the *larval stage* of hackerdom.

Among the first to be known as hackers were professional programmers who, like many technicians, came up with new expressions mainly as a practical shorthand. Now virtually all skilled and obsessive computer users are called hackers (as opposed to *neep-neeps,* who may be merely obsessive). Naturally among the millions of wired minds *(netheads)* across the networks, thousands are creating novel if often sophomoric terminology; and on networks, any novel expression instantly stimulates the community of *neophiliacs*—people who embrace the new. So the vocabulary grows at warp speed. *The New Hacker's Dictionary* (MIT), from which most examples here are taken, had gathered more than three thousand neologisms by its second edition in 1993, including borrowings, shifted meanings, technical terms, and slang. With the explosion of Internet communications since then, the number of generally shared terms has probably doubled. As for the increase in specialized discussion-group or "listserv" terms—who can even guess?

Eric S. Raymond, editor of the dictionary's second edition, coined a number of terms himself; *raster burn* is one and describes the state of eyeballs exposed too long to a monitor's flickering lines of pixels. Not every victim of raster burn, one should note, is a *computer geek*, which the dictionary defines as "one who fulfills all the dreariest negative stereotypes about hackers: an asocial, malodorous, pasty-faced monomaniac with all the personality of a cheese grater." With such less-than-impartial definitions, the dictionary turns up hundreds of spunky terms that invite use outside cyberspace, among them, *farkled*, or messed-up, and *spooge*, an inexplicable or arcane code. Preadolescent expressions such as *baud barf* also abound. Many of the terms already have a foot in the door of standard dictionaries; for example, *phreaking*, or cracking a phone network to make free calls, and *flaming*, massive on-line castigation of a *netiquette* violator.

Rummaging in the Pits

Except at their conventions, the wine, computer, and cuisine cultures raise little more racket than the sounds of clinks, clicks, and digestive growls. A few areas of special expression make up for such quietude. At the Chicago Mercantile Exchange, the baying of some four thousand pit brokers, traders, and runners on a busy day sounds like home-run mania at the ballpark. And yet most of the trading information is communicated by silent hand signals—sign language that can indicate a brokerage house (e.g., neck-rubbing for *Pain*e Webber), desire to buy or sell (palm facing toward or away from body), price offering (fingers and fist in varying positions), and so on. Why the explosive shouting? It has to do with getting one's sign language noticed first, especially when bids or offers are equal.

The pit has its own verbal idiom, too, part of the larger, supercharged jargon of the financial world. In *High Steppers, Fallen Angels, and Lollipops,* Kathleen Odean revels in the folklore of more than five hundred slang terms of Wall Street, some of them old but most still sharp-edged.[2] *High steppers* are fashionable stocks, *fallen angels* glorious stocks that have hit hard times, and *lollipops* a company's generous buy-back of shares to foil a takeover attempt. But there are spikier terms here to be borrowed, even if some of them no longer stimulate the Street's hardened insiders. Here are a dozen I have jotted down (with simplified definitions) from Odean and others:

take a flutter: Make a small speculative purchase.

copper a tip: Do just the opposite of what a confidential tip advises.

standing on velvet: Having made a financial killing.

bisexuai offer: A merger offer featuring a target company whose directors are neither friendly nor unfriendly to a take-over attempt.

floor animals: Traders with an instinct for success.

killer bees: Experts retained by a **sleeping beauty** (takeover target) to resist the **black knight** corporate raiders.

goose job: Buying outstanding shares at increasing prices to force up a price and create an illusory stock **bubble.**

vulture funds: "Dead" real estate snapped up for later profit.

body rain: What an executive fears in bad times: walking the streets looking for work while other bodies are falling from windows.

Scoping for Word Action

Another high-decibel lexicon is that of America's undergraduates, whose neologisms and adaptations of slang from other subcultures range from the brilliant to the intellectual equivalent of a panty raid. *College Slang 101,* a 1972–89 collection by professor and linguist Connie Eble, shows remarkable durability even in the mid-nineties.[3] Could it be that if word patterns are yawped loudly and beerily enough they stick to the universe? A rummage through *101* finds these twenty oldies and many more that are still golden on campus and beyond:

action: Activity. "Ready for some food action?"

dude: Person. "The pizza dude is here."

butt—: Large quantity. "A buttload of money."

weird out: Feel oddly affected. "I was weirded out by her suicidal rap."

blow off: Forget, ignore, skip. "I had to blow off class this morning."

vibes: Inaudible, telling emissions. "The vibes were good, so we dated."

monge out: Overeat, from *manger*. "It's free, kids, so monge out."

airhead: Unaware, vacant person. "Can you explain it to this airhead?"

space cadet: Airhead. Also, the adjectives **clueless** and **ditzy.**

wasted: Drunk. "We were wiped out, wrecked, wasted."

eighty-six: To cut off an intoxicated drinker. "You're eighty-sixed, pal."

outta here: "I'm leaving."

ralph: To vomit. "He ralphed just outside the bar." Also **blow chunks.**

from hell: Good or bad, but heavy-duty. "It's the course from hell."

hunk: Handsome, well-built male. "Killer hunks! Hunks from hell."

cut me some slack: Stop pressuring me. "Cut me some slack on the sex thing, will you?"

cop a tude: React with an unwelcome attitude. "I ask you to cut me some slack and you cop a tude? Outta here."

Trend-driven college expression is quick to label people who fall a step behind the latest cry, or who act conspicuously with-it. Eble lists *earth muffins* and *heywows* in the left-behind category. Activists who wear stylish rebel fashions earn the charming blend word *trendinistas*.

Special Patterns

Occasions such as condemnation and entertainment give rise not only to specialized words, but to modular patterns that can be plugged in as needed. Here, for example, is a module for trashing politicians:

> [fill in the name:]_____, . . . far and away the most miserable, miserly, scheming political miscreant ever to sup and slurp at the public trough while unjustly enriching himself through the petty, brackish alliances the second rate invariably tend to forge in the crucibles of political power.

Warren Hinckle thus described Richard Nixon in a 1994 issue of *Argonaut,* Hinckle's (then) new muckraking quarterly, but the attack pattern and vocabulary are suitable for broader use. Those engaged in public debate must keep an eye out for the modules that will serve them. Here is another:

> It would be highly inappropriate for somebody running a public institution in a democratic society, which I am, to set myself up as a dictatorial arbiter as to who is a serious researcher.

Librarian of Congress James Billington used these words in a 1993 press statement after opening Justice Thurgood Marshall's donated papers to such dubious "researchers" as journalists. Terms like *dictatorial arbiter* help deflect loaded verbiage back to the accusers. Billington had to parry such potshots as *indiscriminate, betrayed, violated, undermined, arrogance, disrespect,* and *gross disregard for the truth,* all contained in a brief op-ed piece by a pair of law clerks who had served Marshall *(The New York Times,* May 27, 1993). Somehow the attackers had left out *malignant, corrosive,* and *national disgrace in the shadow of the Capitol,* the last always applicable in Washington.

Language for Lovers

Sincerity is rarely at question in hostile expression. Hostility has become so natural that we assume the words are meant, whether fresh or borrowed. The statement "I hate your stinking guts," as unoriginal as it may be, is assumed to come from the heart and certainly goes to the heart no matter how many times used. But the language of courtship is different. "I love the twinkle in your eyes" is in trouble immediately as a cliché. Does it come from the heart? Doubtful. Too facile, too generic; it could apply to a pet cockatoo. Does it go to the heart? No, unless the recipient is so desperate for affection that even "You ain't half as ugly as I first thought" weakens the knees.

Love, then, is not an area of easily borrowed modules, except perhaps in greeting-card country, where the thought of someone spending two dollars might sweeten the generic message. For winning hearts, borrowed language is risky; but so is expression that strains for originality. In nascent relationships one walks a narrow line between the stimulating and sentimental, the turn-on and turn-off.

There does exist a heightened, specialized language of love, one that can be raided once uncovered. Most of it lies outside of love-quote collections, whose pearls soon become too familiar to be special. Familiarity also taints such celebrated models as *The Song of Solomon* and the Shakespearian love sonnets, or at least dulls their best-known lines. The most raidable language can be sought in lesser-known sources: literary love tales, published correspondence between lovers both articulate and inflamed, and love poetry—bearing in mind the adage that "bad poetry is always sincere." Avoid cleverness and paeans to beauty in your borrowings. Seek artful expression that lends *precision*—not necessarily art or gild—to your specific love situation. A borrowed word can be made your own, but borrowed phrases should be acknowledged even in informal use; your sensitivity in selecting them is testimony enough to your love.

Below are some samples of passionate lovespeak. If your beloved hasn't encountered them, they may be worth raiding. But only you can judge whether these or other rummagings will suit your heartthrob's background and sensitivities, as well as the situation in which they are delivered. If he or she is disposed to literary expression, and the night is "filled with murmurs, perfumes, and the music of wings,"[4] these could be modules that stimulate:

> [There sits my beloved . . .]
> Laughing Love's low laughter. Oh this, this only
> Stirs the troubled heart in my breast to tremble,
> For should I but see you a little moment,
> Straight is my voice hushed;
> Yea, my tongue is broken, and through and through me
> 'Neath the flesh, impalpable fire runs tingling:
> Nothing do my eyes see, and a noise of roaring
> Waves sounds in my ears;
> Sweat runs down in rivers, a tremor seizes
> All my limbs and paler than grass in autumn,
> Caught by pains of menacing death, I falter,
> Lost in the love trance.
> —Sappho of Lesbos, *Ode,* from the Greek,
> early sixth century B.C.

The florid outbursts, politically incorrect sentiments, and antiquated syntax of older works may not appeal to all beloveds. But the stock images—love as light, for example—have been so

stunningly developed over the centuries as to demand re-
cycling. Depending on the loved one's tastes, the metaphors
might serve anew.

> What other woman could be loved like you,
> Or how of you should love possess his fill?
> After the fulness of all rapture still,—
> As at the end of some deep avenue
> A tender glamour of day—there comes to view
> Far in your eyes a yet more hungering thrill,—
> Such fire as Love's soul-winnowing hands distil
> Even from his inmost ark of light and dew.
> —Dante Gabriel Rossetti, from *Soul-Light*

Every day you find some new way to fan my ardor.
> —Pietro Bembo, letter to Lucrezia Borgia, 1503[5]

Yes, as you guess, Ellen, I am having a bad attack of you just
at present.
> —George Bernard Shaw to Ellen Terry, June 1897

. . . And now! Now I have *You To Love!* You Miracle for
whom I looked and looked these eons upon eons! You
whom I can never love enough! The reach always exceeding
the grasp! You Heart! Clean and strong and free and proud!
My mate!

Surely I am blest among women—having such a
mate—one who calls to the highest in me, and to a
something yet to be that is higher still!

You mate-man! What a challenge you are to your mate-
woman! Oh Carl—Carl—Carl!
> —Lilian Steichen to Carl Sandburg, 1908[6]

You are my Other Self—a complement. I might say love and
kissings and everything that is fond and passionate to you. I
might use all the superlatives of language and every caress
that short Saxon words will carry to you. You are the most

beautiful, graceful woman in the world, the most splendidly equipped of heart, intellect, and feeling, in all the world.—Yet through and over all this . . . some spirit of You . . . always mantling me day and night . . . pure and near and certain—it is this that has made me sob like a foolish child. . . . Always, always, you throw around me that mantle of a glory worth living in and living for—your heart.

—Carl Sandburg to Lilian Steichen, 1908

> Failing to fetch me at first keep encouraged,
> Missing me one place search another
> I stop somewhere waiting for you.
> —Walt Whitman, from "Song of Myself"
> in *Leaves of Grass*

Language not intended as words of courtship can also be borrowed for one's amorous purposes. Sent to me long ago in a Spanish translation, these same lines of Whitman softened the anguish of lovers a continent apart. As romance languages tend to do, the Spanish seems to lend melody. Grab a guitar and tell your lover:

> No te desalientes si no me encontraras,
> Si me perdieras en un lugar,
> buscame en otro.
> En algún lugar te espero.

Take My Words—Please!

Enough of love and its sweet anguish. What about entertainment? What about funny? You want funny? Help yourself to the huge public-domain vocabulary of humor. If ever a special language was born to be raided, it is the prattle of clowns, patterns that seem funnier the more they are stolen and reworked in the manic chop-shops of comedic minds. Although a style that breaks the mold may be the howl of the day, we find comfort and relief in age-old patterns, some of them traceable to the conventions of seventeenth-century Wit, some to medieval Jewish humor such as the Purim *shpils* based on Biblical tales, some to the *goyische shtick* of ancient Greece, some to—

[Plotnik's verbiage is interrupted:]
If you bring that sentence in for a fitting, I can have it shortened by Wednesday.

Oops—I deserved that crack, which is borrowed from an episode of *M*A*S*H* in which the character Hawkeye reacts to a soldier's breathless narrative. The gag is a kind of metaphor, a fanciful association that tickles us. "Your sentence is like a suit that needs tailoring," Hawkeye is saying. But he says it indirectly, allowing us the pleasure of making the connection. And now, of course, I have massacred the gag by dissecting it, since comedy often depends on catching the audience off guard and "fooling" the mind. The most common pattern in modern humor is fooling by indirection. The comic pulls us one way like a wagonload of gullible kids and suddenly jerks us another. Even puns are indirections, jerking us at the last minute to a word's second or buried meaning. But there are infinitely more types:

The important thing in acting is to be able to laugh and cry. If I have to cry, I think of my sex life. If I have to laugh, I think of my sex life.
—Glenda Jackson

Most comic patterns are actually figures of speech, the rhetorical devices developed in ancient drama. Classical comedy took them to absurd extremes. Three figures alone—*hyperbole* (exaggeration), *litotes* (understatement), and *prosopopoeia* (personification of inanimate objects)—must account for half of what we laugh at:

> In the sitcom *Married with Children*, slovenly Al Bundy is asked if he knows what special occasion this is. He guesses wrong. No, says wife Peggy, *this is the night the rest of your body secedes from your armpits.*

> The late British satirist Peter Cook wrote a sketch featuring Dudley Moore as a one-legged actor auditioning for the role of Tarzan. Cook, playing the producer, had to inform poor Tarzan regretfully that he was *deficient in the leg division, to the tune of one.*

> Mark Leyner, gonzo literary comic, refers in interviews to his "codependent dog." Writing about himself, he mixes *bdelygmia* with other figures: *I'm just the cream-soda-swilling, crotch-scratching, irascible, coughing-up-indigestible-bits-of-grizzle-from-some-meat-on-a-stick, surly, greasy, overalls-over-candy-colored-latex-mini-komono . . . don't-bother-me-till-halftime kind of guy that society has made me.*[7]

The celebrated Jewish mother, in many respects the universal mother, is a master of exaggeration, understatement, *irony, significatio* (signifying more than one says), and *mestasis* (offhanded mention of a subject as if it were unimportant). *Don't bother driving me, I'll take a cab.* To this mother everything is *a crime.* No trip to the store is painless, no act concise: *I stood for the bus. I waited. I rode. A hundred stops they made. I schlepped. I looked. I shopped. They had nothing. I bought. I spent. I carried. I dragged. I lugged. . . .*

In *Jewish as a Second Language*, former stand-up comedienne Molly Katz presents standard patterns of motherly significatio and their translations; example: "What a fudge cake! You must have put in a pound of butter!" Translation: "I'm going to be up all night with diarrhea."[8]

• • •

We laugh at patterns that push an uncomfortable situation to a cartoonish extreme. Bill Bryson, adept at the bizarre image, plays upon the anxiety travelers feel in strange and possibly hostile environments. On a Swiss train he overhears a pair of brutal Australian males just out of his sight. They seem to be "serious psychopaths, in urgent need of a clinic." He expects that on spotting him the two will hold his ankles and watch his head bounce on the railway ties. After all, "they were saying things like, 'D'ya remember the time Muscles Malloy beat the crap out of the Savage triplets with a claw hammer? . . . I was picking pieces of brain out of my beer! . . . Yeah, it was fantastic! D'ya remember that time Muscles rammed that snooker cue up Jason Brewster's nose and it came out the top of his head. . . . Did you ever see him eat a live cat?' 'No, but I saw him pull the tongue out of a horse once.' " Eventually Bryson catches a glimpse of the pair, only to learn that "they were both about four feet two inches tall."[9]

Cruelty can be funny when outlandish enough to be satirical, that is, ballooned out to reveal its folly. In comedy as with tragedy, we can experience a catharsis or purging that follows emotional agitation. From a safe distance we are stirred up and eased down by the suffering of the comic victim—as when a sadistic instructor begins a bewildered immigrant's first English lesson with the line "I will feed your fingertips to the wolverines!" (Michael O'Donoghue to John Belushi on *Saturday Night Live*, 1975).

• • •

The most enduring comic patterns become formulas, which can stimulate ideas by providing themes for variation. One of the most persistent stand-up formulas is the *j'ever* pattern, the one that sets up a schtick on the small follies and ironies of life. "J'ever talk to your face in the mirror? *Hi. . . . You're cute in the morning."* "J'ever wonder why men's trousers have an open-ing with sharp, interlocking teeth? *Eeyii!"* With its sly observa-tions on the commonplace, the j'ever pattern is a nutty cousin to lyric poetry. Here's Bobbie Frost, poet and club comic: "J'ever notice how two roads diverge in a wood and, schmucks that we are, we take the one less traveled by? No wonder we're on unemployment. Thank you!" Many of Woody Allen's gags follow the formula of juxtaposition: the serious next to the absurd; the cosmic paired with the mundane. "I keep won-dering if there is an afterlife, and if there is will they be able to break a twenty?" "Whoever shall not fall by the sword or by famine shall fall by pestilence, so why bother shaving?"

Raiding formulas of juxtaposition, indirection, and other de-vices is easy. Filling them in with new levels of incongruity, absurdity, and surprise, however, is a prospect that can lead to head-banging despair. Moreover, the vocabulary of comedy will always vary according to the culture and disposition of an audience. While comedians theorize that certain words and even numbers are inherently funny, while much of slang is funny in its rebelliousness, there are few universals for general audiences. Trying for sarcasm, I might say, "I'm funny like there are people on the moon." But then comes a survey claiming that a third of the nation believes people have always been on the moon. On *Seinfeld,* television's most popular com-edy at this writing, Seinfeld's buddy George concocts a bizarre seduction scheme for his friend and asks, "Do you ever get down on your knees and thank God you have access to my dementia?" Studio laughter explodes; but how many thou-sands of viewers take offense?

Considering that most humor degrades someone or some cherished value, will *anything* be funny as society grows more sensitive to language? Or should one avoid the cutting vocabu-lary of comedy as many academic and workplace communica-tors have soberly resolved to do? This will all depend on whom you wish to stimulate, how, where, and at what price. Swinishness may simply be a habit you need to break.

If it is me you're stimulating, however, and I know you mean only to delight, I am more attentive to another habit. It is what critic Walter Kerr calls a "wonderfully light-footed habit of stepping off a joke before it begins to complain." In the business of comedy, Godzillas need not apply.

14

Speaking Louder than Words: Oral Presentation

*F*ifty:forty:ten. When textbooks approach the topic of face-to-face communications, this old ratio comes up like a sigh of steam. The "fifty" tells us that facial and body language account for more than fifty percent of a listener's emotional stimulation. Some forty percent of the response is triggered by nonverbal vocal qualities such as pitch and volume. And words themselves? An impact factor of ten percent or less.[1] So why, you might ask with wild gestures and *aarrrrghs*, have we been wasting our time thinking about *words,* unless writing is our sole concern?

Better to ask, why do words score so low when listener responses are measured? My answer: Because the words most people speak are dead on arrival—barely worth their ten percent. In earlier chapters we looked at some of the numbing verbiage that dominates our lives. When we hear people saying, "It was determined to identify, develop, and implement multiple training plans for internal and external opportunities," no wonder we're watching for a twitch, hiccup, *anything* to stir an emotional response.

While the power of nonverbal language cannot be denied, these generalized ratios underrate the force of good words themselves. Another oft-heard measure is the twenty-five-percent efficiency with which the average person listens to a speaker. Because the brain can process roughly 600 words a minute and speakers deliver only some 150, we do drift off looking for messages to fill the space. But give me a minute of inventive, startling language instead of predictable mush, and I'm yours one hundred percent. In the audio version of his *Darkness Visible: A Memoir of Madness,* William Styron reads at a careful literary pace, allowing us ample time to think about the day's errands. But we don't wander off, because the language—*besotted, chimera, equipoise, simulacrum, juiceless shuffling remnant*—grips us by the nape.

Not to knock communications-related research, but it tends to draw attention from the true means of mastering oral expression: training in language and practice in oratory. Recently, a reference to a macabre piece of research drew my own attention.[2] Experiments, it seems, were being performed on cadavers to study how breath affects the speaking voice:

> *Method:* Using electric-fan devices, the researchers blew air at varying intensities between the vocal chords of the deceased. *Object:* To demonstrate that force of breath affects the volume level of the speaking voice. *Observation:* Creating suction, the air stream caused the chords (more accurately folds, or bands) of the larynx to meet at various points along their length and emit a buzzing noise or "phonation," the pure, unarticulated sound of vibrating folds. The greater the quantity of air passing between the folds, the louder and more intense the buzz from the dead. *Conclusion:* Breath affects volume and intensity of speech sound.

(Speculation: When no one was looking, the researchers created a barbershop quartet from hell.)

I think of that experiment when I buzz meaninglessly at people or suffer the buzzing of others. Most of the time we speak like corpses. The golden age of oration appears to be long gone. I have little doubt that past orators were more eloquent and forceful than most $25,000-a-shot keynoters. Perhaps without media training a Demosthenes or Frederick Douglass would have bombed on television, yet one longs for a sound bite or two from their likes.

With oratory and elocution no longer embedded in curricula, speech training comes sporadically if ever to most American lives. Parental coaching only strengthens the adolescent resolve never to be intelligible. If we are lucky, a course here, a pep talk there moves us a step closer to oral expressiveness. Advice on forceful language in general, as in earlier chapters of this book, can nudge us further. But as rhetoricians have said for more than two thousand years, forceful language *plus* oral-presentation skills makes for the most powerful expression. Language plus physical thrust delivers thoughts louder than language alone—at least for the short term. Below, we look at certain key attitudes and skills in the sprawling area called Speech.

Sins of the Presenters

These days orators are called presenters, a name they share with models who present prizes on game shows. Speaking at any presentation, from workshop to convocation, gets you the title. Over the years, between performances of my own, I've watched some nine hundred presenters step up to a podium and open their mouths. Perhaps two hundred proceeded to do something stimulating or gave it a brave try. As for the rest, put it this way: I usually root for people's success. But when exposed to speakers so inconsiderate, so callously inept that they violate the very *chi* of their listeners, I must sweep them offstage with an imaginary water cannon. Often their sins are attitudinal; they could take a lesson in *bonhomie* from their game-show counterparts. Below you might recognize, as part of your own past torment, some of the top ten characteristics of People Who Should Be Banned from Presenting.

These people:

- Show no liking for us listeners, who were so ready to like *them.* All we ask is a welcoming, five-second smile just before the opening; an appreciative greeting; and eye contact with particular audience members now and then. Instead, from the start they avert their eyes as if to conceal their *schadenfreude,* their pleasure in our misfortune.

- Speak for an hour or more. No one, not even Fidel Castro, should speak for longer than thirty minutes at a stretch. Most research points to twenty minutes as the maximum gulp of modern audiences. Thirty minutes—plus a twenty-minute Q&A session if Qs are popping—will satisfy any longing for speechification. But program planners mulishly demand an hour's presentation, perhaps to get their honorarium's worth, and speakers agree to this oppressive length.

- Flaunt their unpreparedness. Prepare? Do Gods prepare? Imperiously they shuffle their papers and squint at them as if for the first time. They murmur such rudenesses as "Let's see . . . what shall we talk about today?" or "Bear with me if you've heard my remarks at other conferences." They make no reference to the particular audience.

- Show no mercy. Sound systems fail, thermostats freeze, timers go off; they show no interest. "I don't need a microphone" is a common opener that brings gloom. A presenter has the power to relieve discomfort and anxieties: "Can everyone hear me? Can someone get the heat turned up? I promise to conclude within three minutes."

- Undermine their authority. They inform us: "I'm no expert on this topic. In fact, I didn't know it existed until yesterday; but maybe over the next hour I'll hit on something you haven't heard. . . ."

- Fail to brief themselves on the achievements and sensitivities of the audience. "What have we here, librarians? I've always said you've got the best buns in the business. But then I guess I'm one of those people you like to shush."
- Branch off from the desired topic. Brief digressions can be refreshing, but pointless branching is a hostile act. Listeners despair of ever getting home when branchers set off like this:

I believe that the future—and I see that everyone is in the prediction business—of course, business of any sort is risky today; do you know that small-business operators now have to pay health insurance on every last employee? No wonder we hire illegal aliens. When my parents immigrated from Sweden—well, I'll come back to that, but let's talk about Scandinavia in the first place. Beautiful scenery. But you pay twelve dollars for half a sandwich. Know what's on it? I'll tell you. . . .

- Employ deadening visual aids and props. Who ever thought that overhead projections *aid* anything besides an audience's escape in the dark? Even when handled seamlessly, which they rarely are, aids and props tend to steal from expressiveness. Boring figures and textual outlines are no less boring projected on a screen or dolled up with computer graphics. In fact, why does anyone want to *orate* tables, graphs, and outlines? Probably because visual aids make it possible. But these sleep-inducing images are hardly the stuff of human expression.

Pictorial slides or video clips have their place, but should take up no more than half the time of a presentation. Enliven the other half with the expressiveness of words, voice, and gesture flowing through mind and body, colored and textured by those remarkable devices. Theoretically, the eighty muscles of the face alone can produce some seven thousand expressions.[3] Try beating that with presentation slides.

- Stress us with stressful behavior. What does it say when a presenter rocks like a metronome, hyperventilates through the text without glancing up or pausing, and wears a pair of ruts into the sides of the podium? It says the presenter could not be bothered with the first principles of public speaking, available in virtually any primer (see Resources) and attainable with moderate practice; briefly:

A. Stance: Establish a basic position, weight forward on both feet; step deliberately out of the position from time to time, but return to it. Relax but don't scrunch the upper body and constrict breathing.

B. Working with text: (1) Look at someone in the audience and speak; (2) pause; look down, and get the next chunk of words in mind; (3) look at someone in the audience and speak. Don't speak at length looking down. Use only the top half of your pages for text.

C. Movement: Keep hands free to gesture and to turn or slide your pages. (Don't reveal a big heap of papers.) Make smooth but deliberate movements timed to key words. Gesture well above the podium or move to the side of it; use overstated gestures for larger audiences, understated for intimate audiences and television.

• Finally, these presenters make no attempt to modulate the voice. Most (Anglo) Americans are notorious droners. It may take a supernatural effort to overcome one's habitual monotone. It may feel grossly unnatural—but rarely does it project as such to an audience. On the contrary, audiences will cherish any effort: key words picked out in advance for a leap in pitch, an occasional theatrical exaggeration of tone, an imitation of some character's inflected speech. But amateur speakers are so afraid of appearing odd, they stick with the buzz of cadavers. Get those electric fans!

In his appearances and videotapes, speaking consultant Arch Lustberg calls ''likability'' the most important objective for speakers. He talks about an ''open'' face, a welcoming and likable face, with eyebrows raised slightly and facial lines horizontal. He makes a very funny "dead face" that we all recognize. Neither ghoulish faces nor the sins we've mentioned make communication mechanically impossible, but when they cause an audience to dislike you, you might better have called in sick.

Vocal and Nonvocal Projection

A world of communicative "behavior" complements spoken words. Linguists differ, I have noticed, in the way they classify the elements of such behavior—elements such as volume, rhythm, pitch, and gesture. They group them variously under such terms as *intonation, suprasegmentals, prosodic features,* and *paralanguage,* pretty words if sometimes soft around the edges. But we can't worry about semantic boundaries here. We face enough challenge managing all the vocal and nonvocal "cues" that color our spoken words, especially if these cues are dominating our perceived messages.

So let's settle for a loose understanding: *Segments* are the vowels and consonants that make up vocalized syllables and words; *how* we vocalize them is the stuff of *suprasegmental* analysis, which studies *prosodic features,* or the communicative effects of pitch, volume, stress, speed, and rhythm of speech. We can think of *paralanguage* as the messages inherent in tone (voice quality), variations from standard pronunciation, and nonlinguistic utterances such as sighs. According to some definitions, paralanguage includes the messages of nonvocal behavior, such as facial and body expression and silent pauses.

These are terms and elements to be contemplated in tranquillity, never as you address an audience. Worry about suprasegmentals as you speak and you could end up talking in tongues—an interesting paralinguistic behavior but usually off the point. We do not need to fret about the "cueing" elements that accompany words; we do need to think about them before performing; we want to practice techniques that help manage them, get them to work for us, and build our confidence. After all, in oratorical skills most of us are at ground zero. We are prisoners of bad habits, all those old mousey, slack-jawed, or motor-mouthed patterns. We generally lack the theatrical training to magnify (project) our conversational voices and gestures so that they appear life-size to an audience; we have barely acknowledged the range of expression available in our voices and gestures.

Well, we've been busy. But once we are ready to improve, even baby steps in the way of *projection* or *variety* will add force to our messages, distinguishing us from gross amateurs. For starters, consider the following few basic prosodic (and para-linguistic) elements and, under "Tips," what to do about each:

Shout and Sing: Elements of Prosody

Volume. Loudness or faintness of voice. Volume is a function of air pushing through the larynx (voice box), where it triggers vibration of the vocal folds (or "chords" or "bands"). The sustained volume of a presentation, even with a microphone, requires an adequate supply of forceful air—much more so than in softer, broken conversation. This means full breathing to fill the lungs. For the infrequent presenter, an hour of intense volume will irritate the vocal chords; gradual buildup in rehearsals will adapt them to speaking conditions.

> *Tips:* Moderate training and practice in uniform breathing, from the "center" of the body, will mitigate the panting-puppy effect. Stomach moves out, diaphragm moves away from the lungs on the big intake; abdominal muscles contract gently as air is pushed through the voice box. Assertive volume enlivens a presentation. When has a presenter seemed too loud? But varied levels work magic,

as in this combo: a statement at medium volume; a shouted repetition; an enforcing whisper into a mike. "Let freedom ring. . . . LET FREEDOM RING! . . . *Let freedom ring.*"

Pitch. Your voice as measured by notes on a musical scale, low to high. Everyday range: about an octave. The male voice reaches full maturity in pitch at about age twenty-five; the female voice, thirty-five. In our *intonation system* we use pitch and melody to signal meanings, to put a spin on our verbal messages. Gradual change of pitch within a word or syllable is called *inflection.* [Ralph, with rising pitch:] "Alice, one of these *days . . .*" [Alice, falling pitch:] "Awww, *Ra*alph. Ya *poo*or slob." Abrupt changes between words or larger elements are called *steps.* "Norton—you mailed it *when?*"

> *Tips:* Don't affect someone else's low or high voice. Find your most comfortable *(habitual)* pitch, one that allows for easy volume; then work on gradually expanding your range so that your speech is more inflected—high for emotional emphasis, low for gravity, melodic for certain dramatic effects, as in storytelling. Use your normal octave fully; go beyond it for effect, as in "Good *morn*ing" to workshop participants *("morn"* jumping twelve to sixteen whole tones above the "good"). Mark key words in your speech script with your own musical notation. Review yourself on tape to avoid repetitive, monotonous, or whining patterns.

Voice Quality. Adult or childish? Stentorian or reedy? Chief executive officer or pismire? The dynamics of voice quality include: the physical structure of the larynx, which you can't do anything about; *phonation,* the creation of *tone* as moving air vibrates the vocal folds; and *resonation,* the amplification and shaping of sound in the cavities of the throat and head—the pharynx, mouth, and nasal cavity (see figure). If you can execute a convincing moo, meow, and woof-woof, you are using the cavities well. Separating oral and nasal cavities is the *velum,* or soft palate at the back of the oral roof. On the "meow" you can feel it lowering to allow sound to resonate in the nose cave.

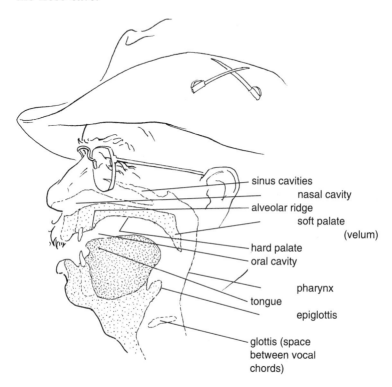

sinus cavities
nasal cavity
alveolar ridge
soft palate
(velum)
hard palate
oral cavity
pharynx
tongue
epiglottis
glottis (space
between vocal
chords)

Rough riding the speech organs. "I feel like a bull moose!" said Theodore Roosevelt returning from the Spanish-American War. To resonate those words, he used air cavities in the chest, larynx, pharynx, nose, sinuses, and mouth interior; to articulate them, he enlisted tongue, teeth, lips, alveolus (upper gum ridge), hard palate, soft palate (velum), and, being Teddy Roosevelt, plenty of jaw.

Tips: Drink extra water the day before a talk. The day you speak, avoid milk, coffee, alcohol, whispering, shouting, and excessive throat clearing, all of which can foul the larynx. Drink decaffeinated tea. The pharynx—what the doctor sees when you say "ahhh"—affects tightness of voice by its muscular hardening and softening. Mix it up: Relax to achieve mellowosity; tighten to portray evil, disgust. Lazy control of resonation sends vowels through the nose, especially after the nasals *m*, *n*, and *ng*. Open the mouth wider and direct the resonation away from the velum, toward the front of the mouth. You should feel the resonance shift back to the nose on the last word of this phrase: "Man, you don't know *beans.*"

Articulation has to do with distinguishing connected parts of speech. To articulate means to utter the individual segments distinctly, so that the consonants, vowel sounds, and syllables are clear even when joined at high speed. The main articulating instruments (for English) are lips, jaws, teeth, velum, and the tongue as it humps, curls, and interacts with the palate and other parts of the mouth. These instruments carve words out of sound. Dulling them creates familiar effects: lazy jaw and lips = Valley talk; lazy tongue and velum = potato-mouth. Extreme articulation may sound prissy, but pronounced consonants, formed by restricting or interrupting the air stream, mark careful speech.

> *Tips:* Exercise those articulators! Listen to yourself on tape. Do you articulate the *th* in *clothes?* The *sts* in *mists?* Each syllable and the rounded *o* in *mirror?* If not, slow down. Repeat Nabokov's opening of *Lolita:* ". . . the tip of the tongue taking a trip of three steps down the palate to tap, at three, on the teeth. Lo. Lee. Ta." Articulation simply calls for all the sounds that belong in the connected words. "Do you realize that your government seized one thousand diamonds in February?" Use extra stress for dramatic emphasis—"*ssseeezeduh* one thousand diamonds"—and when you practice to loosen up those frozen articulators. Focus on consonants. Speech primers offer enunciation exercises to expedite excellence.

Speed, Phrasing, and Rhythm. Professional speakers deliver about 150 to 170 words a minute, but they vary the *tempo* for effect: Slow for transition, emphasis, gravity, danger, horror. Fast for comedy, urgency, excitement, dynamic action. Nervous amateurs use two gears: fast and frantic, losing much of their articulation, nuance, and audience. *Phrasing* is the delivery of content in distinct units of thought, separated by pauses or other transitions. *Rhythm* is achieved by frequent contrasts, regular and irregular, in tempo, volume, pitch, and other elements, even gesture (as in podium-thumping). Rise in volume and/or pitch *stresses* a syllable or word to create rhythmic contrasts.

> *Tips:* What could be more manageable than planning the varied tempos of your presentation in advance? Identify those passages that are dense with meaning, rich in language, dark in emotion, and mark SLOWER in the margins. These, like (marked) high-speed passages, should be brief, rarely more than half a minute, and well scattered. A reasonable ratio for normal, faster, and slower passages would be 50:35:15; spread them throughout the text for variety. Variety must govern your rhythm as well. Relieve the iambic beat (ba-*boom* ba-*boom)* of normal speech with shifted stress (*let* freedom ring), with playful accents, with lines of non-iambic poetry, with hellfire preaching.

Advice and Imitation

Sigh. All these elements to bear in mind, not to mention those described in earlier chapters—the pause, body language, clothing "statements," and so on. Even if abandoned in most classrooms, techniques of face-to-face expression abound in popular texts, cassettes, and seminars—techniques for toastmasters, broadcasters, educators, actors; for Business People Who Want to Win Every Time; for Couples Who Need to Get Past Sex-Based Differences in Conversation.

Cramming on too many techniques will overwhelm even high achievers. Easy does it, and remember that each technique has its risk factor—the possibility that it will backfire under certain circumstances. Your circumstances. The only certainty of face-to-face expressiveness is that occasionally you will fall on your face. Few things in life feel worse than a disastrous presentation—or better than a winner the next time. Every seasoned presenter has bombed horrendously, has learned from it, and has moved on.

Improvements demand risk and courage, but not necessarily immersion in formal speech training. Many are the oral pipsqueaks who evolved into power speakers mainly by aping the masters. Here, so far, we have touched on some critical elements of speech behavior. Your next assignment—a pleasurable one—is to observe a few master presenters in performance. Ideally, you can rent or record these performances on videotape, pause them, and play them back. Now, with your raised awareness of speech dynamics, you can concentrate on the performer's use of each element: volume, pitch, voice quality, articulation, speed, phrasing, rhythm. Finally, just as the masters do, you can begin mimicking some of the techniques that pay off. Do it until you make them yours.

Monologuist Spalding Gray may not be to everyone's taste, but two factors make him a good study: His videos are widely available, and his vocal equipment is probably no better than yours; in fact, it is flawed—a brassy voice and sputtering lisp. Nevertheless, watch how he takes each element to the outer limits and back. Notice his use of contrast to build tension, surprise, delight. Critic Ben Brantley described a New York performance of *Gray's Anatomy* as a "marvel of modulated craftsmanship," shifting between comic deadpans, "expressionistic wails of a man spiraling out of control, and the babel of diversely rendered voices."[4]

Like the monologue that made Gray's reputation, *Swimming to Cambodia,* his *Monster in a Box* (New Line Home Video, 1992) is a minicourse in expressionistic self-portraiture. Using the elements of voice, face, and body, Gray paints an engagingly neurotic backdrop to such passages as "I think it was a boundary problem. I have very weak boundaries. I think his insanity was leaking into mine." Note the brief, hysterical rhythm here, or as he describes a writer's backslide into drinking: "I drink and I write and I drink and I drink and I drink . . ."; the tempo increases; a bongo marks the rhythm; he pantomimes the action; volume rises; voice tightens—crescendo!

Key to a monologuist's success is the art of narrative: storytelling that takes form, builds momentum, delivers a climax. Any presenter benefits from storytelling skills. Among the most skillful models are professional storytellers whose audiences are usually children. Adults can learn from these masters at libraries and fairs or on video. Recently I watched a young storyteller named André Keit enthrall educators with the simplest of tales, sweeping aside centuries and the walls of the room with his opening words: "Once upon a time in Africa, when stones were soft . . ." Among Keit's techniques: prolonged silent pauses after narrative high points, usually with face frozen in mock emotion; every so often a brief, rhythmic refrain, sung sweetly or whispered; abrupt changes of tempo, volume, and pitch; and shifts in character or diction: "That Br'er Rabbit could—paaar-*tee!*" Keit directed his character's outbursts at individual listeners, so that they, too, became characters in the narrative whether they liked it or not. They loved it. And who were Keit's models? "Red Foxx, Bill Cosby, Whoopi Goldberg, church preachers, and crazy cousins."

Though I've used two males as examples, women actually have the edge in my Speakers Hall of Fame. *Essence* editor-in-chief Susan Taylor, for example, is as stimulating an inspirational keynoter as one will ever cheer. Or watch Gloria Steinem. Julie Andrews. Diana Rigg. Are speaking skills a gender thing? From what I've seen, women's faces are generally more open, their pace less subject to drag. The pitch of women is normally more varied—unless they are trying to sound like men. And listen up, guys: Men who aren't afraid to sound "like a woman" tend to be more animated and likable, without coming off as effete.

All-Day Talkers

A special breed of presenters are the workshop leaders or "facilitators" who try to keep people awake at all-day training sessions. Here the distinguishing skill is *energy* as communicated in the various elements of expression, including language. Energy not only energizes audience members, but signals the presenter's excitement, as if something important were going on. It helps if the performer actually feels this way, but by the twentieth presentation on safety-code compliance the thrill could be gone. Storytelling techniques help maintain the illusion: the animated face; brief narratives that race to a climax; pregnant pauses; engagement with individual members of the audience—ideally by name; emphatic gestures; and aggressive movement throughout the room—including an occasional charge at the audience in the style of Portuguese *fado*.

From one management workshop I picked up a little flamenco-like move that the presenter used to underscore her points. For example, here is how she stressed that in teamwork "it is not the results, it's the process": On the *not* she leaped at the audience, weight on the left foot; on *sults* she dragged the right foot forward to join the left; on *pro* she stepped sideways with the right foot, crouching slightly; and on *cess* she snapped the right foot back to click heels and stand at attention. The message stuck.

In their efforts to project vitality, workshop leaders embrace certain behavioral clichés. Men whip off the jacket, hook it over a shoulder for a while, loosen the tie, roll up the sleeves. Both sexes ask "O*kay?*" as a rhetorical question at the end of every point. Easel pads are attacked furiously with broad marker pens, sheets are torn loose and taped to the walls to display the parade of "exciting" ideas elicited thus far. If the presenter's language and content show some originality, these conventional moves may work yet another time, but intelligent audiences are finding them inane. Either joke about using them or try something new.

The Fear

All speech primers address the fear of public speaking, pointing out that it usually tops death and illness on our lists of dreaded situations. And many are the suggestions for coping with fear, most of them helpful even if made from the safety of someone's writing table. But no advice will eliminate the basic human fear of mass disapproval.

Approval, after all, is what we seek most from a general audience, even more than we seek its understanding of our "points." Most speech counselors fixate on the achievable goal of making just a few points, using simple language, so that listeners "take something away with them." For technical or sales presentations this approach might make sense, and it does lessen the risk of failure; but otherwise, why should listeners drag themselves to my talk, sit for a half hour, and applaud me for my two or three points—points they can acquire more efficiently in an article or live happily without?

When I speak, I approach an audience believing that these listeners want soft stimulation, not hard points. They want *refreshment* from informational communications. They want a pleasant half hour of human touch, of language that touches their own experience in fresh, precise, and evocative ways.

They want expression that can be heard clearly, seen in a variety of actions, and savored during brief pauses. They want to laugh, because it feels good to laugh in a group, but not be compelled to laugh repeatedly at lame humor. With this ambitious approach I virtually eliminate fear and replace it with—terror.

Terror is why I do not accept speaking engagements lightly, and why I rehearse for some six to ten weekends for a half-hour presentation. The only balance to terror is preparation—the knowledge that you have honed every line for delivery to this particular audience, that you have worked every word and phrase through your articulators hundreds of times, and that all your planned emphases, timing, and modulations will survive a double lobotomy and the onstage panic known as "brownout." Other speakers will make their own adjustments, but terror is why I:

- Check out the speaking room, test the mike, learn how to adjust it.
- Bring a complete marked text to the podium, having prepared well enough to maintain eye contact and to ad lib without losing my place.
- Carry an extra copy of the text in case a part is missing.
- At the podium, before speaking, grin three seconds at each of three scattered individuals. (Amazingly, the whole audience smiles back.)
- Open my talk by singing the first few lines or howling out a key word, assuring the audience that I am not here to put them to sleep and immediately breaking the chains of inhibition.
- Do not tell the long, punch-line jokes that make everyone apprehensive.
- Do use reliable ice-breakers such as Hollywood one-liners or farcical voices ("This is your conscience, Arthur!") to ease the way for subtler humor.

- Think of how people applaud the most wooden poetry readings, and how adored I must be for offering language *and* showmanship.
- Show enjoyment, show I'm having fun, even if I'm dying!

These are nine things I do. A tenth is to review my text within the next twenty-four hours, noting what worked, what didn't, and what adjustments can keep the demon Terror at bay. For my next talk I might also pump up with this mantra I found in a guide to "power presentations":

> I feel like taking on whole armies by myself . . .
> I have ten hearts. I have 100 arms.
> I feel too strong to war with mortals.
> Bring me GIANTS![5]

And in Conclusion . . .

In conclusion, ladies and gentlemen, let us return to the beginning—to those ancient masters of rhetoric, who for the sake of oratory perfected the *figures of speech*. The figures of speech. Nothing has exceeded these classical devices as models for stimulating listeners. Review them in this book, study them elsewhere; observe them in use, build them into your own talks.

In writing, certain classical figures may fall out of fashion or seem excessive, but remember, these figures were developed for empowering speech, and they continue to do that job today. Consider *anaphora,* a succession of statements beginning with the same group of words:

> We find common ground at the plant gate that closes on workers without notice. We find common ground at the farm auction where a good farmer loses his or her land to bad loans or diminishing markets. Common ground at the school yard where teachers cannot get adequate pay . . .

Common ground at the hospital admitting room where
someone is dying tonight because they cannot afford . . .
insurance. . . .

The Rev. Jesse Jackson used anaphora and dozens more figures in his "Common Ground" address to the 1988 Democratic Convention in Atlanta. And as he closed he offered these
words, which I pass along to all of you who aspire to expressiveness:

Wherever you are tonight, you can make it. Hold your head
high. Stick your chest out. You can make it.

Thank you.

Afterword:
Putting Thoughts into Digits

Thunder. Enter the three Witches.

> Double, double toil and trouble;
> Fire, burn; and, caldron, bubble.
> Eye of newt, and toe of frog,
> *Up we boot, and on we log!*
> (With apologies to the witches of *Macbeth,* IV:1.)

*A*nd so, cackle, cackle, into the brew of human expression comes cyberspeak, a style of talking on (and about) computer networks—especially the great mother nexus of networks, the Internet.* For most people on the planet, the network medium—known as cyberspace—is a murky ether suited to the spirits of the night. Didn't science fiction writer Arthur C. Clarke observe that "any sufficiently advanced technology is

---

* Some terms: The prefix *cyber* derives from "cybernetics," a 1947 coinage by American Norbert Wiener, who pioneered the study of analogies between living organisms and computers, particularly their control and communication systems. *The Net* is a collective term for the computer networks of cyberspace, and a nickname for the Internet, which links them. *Digital* refers to the binary on-off (1-0) electronic code, the basic language of computers. *Virtual* means replication of the physical world in cyberspace, as in *virtual sex.*

indistinguishable from magic''? Each day as the technologies of interactive computing leap forward, they ensorcell even those who grasped them yesterday.

The word-sorcery that spellbinds literary audiences tends to wilt in cyberspace; the magical force is the technology linking your computer with fifty million others around the globe. As for the tools of expression, they boil down to vernacular fluency, knowledge of a few protocols and conventions (''netiquette''[1]), and a taste for schmoozing with strangers.

Mixed Messages

Does cyberspeak signal the morphing—the quick-melt transformation—of conventional expression into some new digital putty? Not yet. But electronic forces are generating new tools of expression, each competing with well-tempered words for attention. No longer need our three witches summon the language of Shakespeare for effect; with present technology they can express themselves across the worldwide digital networks in all the shapes and forms allowed by text, computer graphics, audio, and video. Not just express themselves, but engage their audience in interactive mischief, eliciting instant feedback.

We hear that by the millennium most of us will be communicating thus, like empowered wizards. We will move easily between the global community and our tight-knit electronic tribes or ''virtual neighborhoods.'' Our language will be telegraphic, coded, fitted more to flying electrons than to stable print.

So. Are we talking miracle or catastrophe? Can thoughts go digital? Will words retain their magic? Will literature survive?

These and broader societal questions are being churned in so many forums and with such anxiety that I have considered hibernating until the verdict is in. One sign of the confusion: The Internet Addiction Support Group, an on-line chat community, spends its time discussing how to break the habit of on-line chatting. Most analysts see a mix of values in the "digital revolution," but few underestimate its impact:

• For Louis Rossetto, the "only parallel is probably the discovery of fire." Rossetto is the force behind *Wired* magazine, a standard-bearer of the revolution, and *Hotwired,* an on-line medium of "way new journalism" reaching hundreds of thousands of "digital savvies." *Hotwired* talks the talk, describing itself as a "cyberstation," containing "a suite of vertical content streams within an integrated community space."[2]

• Douglas Rushkoff offers the term "datasphere" for our "media-fed and media-connected world," including the web of computer networks.[3] In the datasphere, for better or for worse, one spark of information can light a global flame within hours or even minutes.

• How will expression be packaged and consumed? Not in the form of atoms, according to media guru Nicholas Negroponte. Atoms are fixed in time and space; electronic digits can be dispersed and shared. "Content providers" will spew streams of interactive entertainment and educational programming in digital form; no longer will consumers be constrained by what publishers and broadcasters care to package as units. Instead, these consumers—or "broadcatchers"—will use automated "messenger agents" to reel in and manipulate choice digital bits how and when they want them.[4]

• Astronomer Clifford Stoll, hero among hackers after his first book, drew gasps for turning computerphobic in his next. He laments the widespread computer addiction that he says draws people from the stimulating environment of the off-line world and into shallow virtual reality. Among other losses of quality, he observes a dumbing-down of language, often "ungrammatical, misspelled, and poorly organized."[5]

"Cybergripe," scoffs one response to Stoll. Such backlashers, says *New Yorker* reviewer James Gleick, fail to distinguish transi-

tory issues from fundamental ones. "The Internet," says Gleick, "is making the painful transition . . . from a haven for academics and teen hackers to a public utility embracing the general populace." Like all frontier worlds, he says, it will be rude, ugly, and lawless until it sorts itself out.[6]

Network Expression

The network community does seem to be groping for order, even as individuals achieve new levels of rudeness and ugliness, for the freedom to be unidentified on the Net has loosed a number of dark spirits into cyberspace. The crackpots, militants, and stalkers are on the job, and it doesn't take long to meet with cyber-expressiveness from hell. Yet many Net users are as law-abiding as others are barbaric. For example, despite the general sloppiness of cybergrammar, certain groups are fastidious and will flame (attack en masse) an act of carelessness. Try dangling a participle in front of a discussion group most recently residing at **COPYEDITING-L@cornell.edu,** one of several network forums on language usage. On the Internet, even as students engage in electronic food fights, faculty debate in the civilized manner that characterizes their off-line discourse; insensitive language is flamed.

Cyberspeak is heir in general to the style of the scientists, engineers, and programmers who pioneered the Net. That style—at least among adults—runs to the functional, or informational, with flashes of cleverness and wit. Hackers (using the term loosely) stimulate one another with their inventive jargon. *Ops, apps,* and *bots* are as "gardens bright with sinuous rills" to the bards of high tech. But expressiveness of any staying power is rare on the Net, where immediacy rules. Literary virtues such as endurance or resonance are largely irrelevant. In their wide-selling *The Elements of E-mail Style,* technical writers David Angell and Brent Heslop observe:

A generation raised on Strunk and White learned to write in a leisurely way, employing a writing and editing process that often took hours or days. This simply doesn't work for messages in the e-mail medium, where turnaround times are often measured in minutes.[7]

About half this style book, however, recapitulates the principles favored by Strunk and White for conciseness, vitality, and precision. And rightly so; these qualities are priceless in a medium that seems ready to swallow the whole of human verbiage.

Standing Out On-line

We return to the questions, What sort of expression *is* distinctive in cyberspace? How best to put thoughts into bits? I offer only fleeting observations, for even as I write, the Thing that is cyberculture mutates before my eyes. I have no idea what will be out there by the time you read this (but I suspect we will be bloody tired of saying *cyber*).

For on-line communicators the stylistic advice of Strunk, White, Angell, and Heslop will apply, but not that of Longinus, whose *On Great Writing* advised against "excessively concise language." Grandeur, said Longinus, "is maimed when forced into too small a mold." And small indeed is the Net user's attention span, often described as a gnat's breath.

Not that grand expression is absent from cyberspace. One can call up thousands of electronic files of literature, articles, and every imaginable cultural resource. One can browse them, explore sections on screen, or download them into print (still the most readable format). The network community is moving toward the digitization of entire library collections. So the language will be there, on record at least, for those in search of meanings, resonance, and relief from the mundane. Many electronic "sites" offer proving grounds for new writers. At present, the most popular creative expression in cyberspace is graphical, but one can imagine individual authors luring readers to their electronic address on the merit of words alone. And whatever one imagines on the Net has usually happened.

But meanwhile, anyone who can approximate a sentence gets an audience on the Net. As a result, millions of nonwriters who never dreamed of publication are exposing themselves in words. In search of democracy, one finds it here. In search of expressiveness, one appreciates anew the system of screening and editing that characterizes print publishing.

Some observers are pleased to see that reluctant writers, including undergraduates, are finding their way to the written word, discovering the pleasures of correspondence. But it is largely an untutored way, not a revival of epistolary art. In both letter writing and E-mail, words can be delivered without interruption. Letter-writers take that opportunity to order thoughts and slowly craft them into felicitous words to stimulate the correspondent. For many of the E-mailers who exchange one-sentence messages all day, the computer is a neat way to keep people from butting in while you say your cool thing. (And I am not innocent in this respect.)

"Elegance," as valued in the world's great correspondence, is rarely sought in E-expression. In cyberspeak "elegance" refers not to sublime language but to software. An elegant program is one that is graceful, user-friendly, seamless. Elegant writing simply gets lost among the megabytes.

Die, Curmudgeons!

Before the digital revolutionaries line me up against a virtual wall, let me say this: I have no problem with digits. I have no intention of ditching my computer and its network connections. True, cyberspeak is about as appealing to my ear as a Texas marching band playing "Hard Day's Night." But I can take a generous view of on-line communications as a kind of renaissance, especially for a society that has devalued the art of conversation, including the art of listening. On the Net people have developed a format for expressing more than a fragmentary thought and for being heard and answered—often *point by point*. A small miracle. The practice of *discourse*, if not always the art, has been revived. Where but on electronic forums are average people actually discoursing on topics other than their ills and aches? In the ancient world, the art of expressiveness arose in support of discourse, of earnest and thoughtful discussion. Perhaps it will rise again, even on-line.

Right now my own bursts of E-expression offer relief from the strain of off-line expressiveness. Writing E-mail, I need hardly forge a personality in the smithy of my prose; instead, I can belt out words in the one manner that seems to impress on-line correspondents: *instantly*. Let the jargon and vogue words flow; no one will judge them past their shelf lives. In fact, by flying through the here and now, I am freeing my creative right brain from the editorial control of the left—exactly what writing gurus suggest as step one along the path to expressiveness.

A Pound of Advice

"Nothing is worth publishing if it is not of the first intensity," poet Ezra Pound is reported to have said. As noble as the words sound, I was never sure what they meant except that Pound was no publishing accountant. But now in the electronic age the notion of "intensity" gives me a handle on the singularity of "wetware" (what hackers call the brain) working off-line.

Expression of the first intensity is news that stays news, to quote Pound's definition of literature; or words that reverberate in the soul, or thought articulated into wisdom. These are life-sustaining elements of humanity, and traditionally they have issued from wetware chugging away on its own. So far, I have seen little of the first intensity generated in cyberspace. This level of expression is not a product of chat groups or even literary forums. It is not informational. We make our way to it not through network links, but through the most interactive medium ever to be developed in humanspace: the mind.

No lover of stimulating expression need resist the digital revolution *as long as expression of "the first intensity" is not displaced.* Let the digits stream and the broadcatchers catch what they will, as long as somewhere the magic of language is nurtured and preserved. Only through the intensity of crafted language, of thoughts beaten into best words and savored over time, do we transcend the mundane and enter realms of exaltation. People can exist as computers exist, exchanging functional bits. "But what is bumping like a helium balloon at the ceiling of their brain never finds its way out," as Sandra Cisneros puts it. Only when those intensities roiling in our souls take verbal form, their every complexity in focus, are we fully expressed.

Notes

1. Gasping for Words

1. Laurence M. Fisher, "Generational Move Likely at Gallo," *The New York Times*, 5 May 1993, national edition.

3. Grammar and Other Night Sweats

1. Paul Roberts, *Understanding Grammar* (New York: Harper, 1954), 5.
2. Roberts, 321.
3. Arnold Lazarus and H. Wendell Smith, *A Glossary of Literature & Composition* (Urbana, Ill.: National Council of Teachers of English, 1983), 243. The authors also cite *A Generative Rhetoric of the Paragraph* as an example of how the term is suddenly revered.

4. Expressiveness

1. From the sixth edition (published in the expressive sixties) of *Webster's New Collegiate Dictionary*.
2. Vincent van Gogh, Letter 531, September 3, 1888, *Further Letters of Vincent van Gogh to His Brother, 1886–1889* (Boston: Houghton Mifflin, 1929).
3. O. M. Watson and T. D. Graves, "Quantitative Research in Proxemic Behavior," *American Anthropologist* 68(1966) 971–85; quoted in Albert Mehrabian, *Silent Messages*, 2nd. ed. (Belmont, Calif.: Wadsworth, 1981).
4. *The Barnhart Dictionary of Etymology* (New York: H. W. Wilson, 1988).
5. "Despair Haunts Midwest as Water Keeps Rising," *The New York Times*, 24 July 1993, national edition.

5. Steps Toward Expressiveness

1. From Willie Morris, *New York Days* (Boston: Little, Brown, 1993).

6. Expressing "the Real You"

1. Marvin Bell, "Poetry Is a Way of Life, Not a Career," *The Chronicle of Higher Education,* 16 Feb. 1994.

2. Op-Ed page, *The New York Times,* 10 March 1994.

3. At about the same time, in another hideous "statement," Baruch Goldstein massacred some thirty Muslim worshipers in Hebron, Israel, before being beaten to death by survivors. "He wasn't a man of words," his wife reportedly said. "He never spoke much."

4. Leonard Michaels, "The Long Comeback of Henry Roth: Call It Miraculous," *The New York Times Book Review,* 15 Aug. 1993.

5. Mel Gussow, "V. S. Naipaul in Search of Himself: A Conversation," *The New York Times Book Review,* 24 April 1994.

6. From *"Bien* Pretty," in *Woman Hollering Creek and Other Stories,* by Sandra Cisneros (New York: Vintage Books, 1991).

7. Robert Jay Lifton, *The Protean Self: Human Resistance in an Age of Fragmentation* (New York: Basic Books, 1994). In Greek mythology, Proteus was Neptune's herdsman and could change into any shape, any object, at will. Protean thus means readily taking on different forms or aspects, ever-changing.

8. Felicia R. Lee, "Grappling with How to Teach Young Speakers of Black Dialect," *The New York Times,* 5 Jan. 1994.

7. Elements of Force

1. *The Mask,* film directed by Charles Russell, 1994.

2. Elizabeth Barrett Browning, "How Do I Love Thee," *Sonnet XLIII, from the Portuguese,* 1850.

3. Steven Pinker, *The Language Instinct* (New York: William Morrow, 1994).

4. Xenophon, *Memoirs of Socrates.*

5. James Joyce, *Portrait of the Artist as a Young Man* (New York: Viking, 1956).

6. Heinrich Böll, *And Never Said a Word,* translated by Leila Vennewitz (Chicago: Northwestern University Press, 1994).

7. Tom Wolfe, *Mauve Gloves and Madmen, Clutter and Vine, and Other Stories, Sketches, and Essays* (New York: Farrar, Straus, and Giroux, 1976).

8. Craig M. Carver, "Word Histories," *Atlantic Monthly,* January 1944.

9. Larry McEnerney, "Hard Copy," *University of Chicago Magazine,* February 1994.

10. Geoffrey Whelan quoted in "Rocking in Shangri-La," by John Seabrook, *The New Yorker*, 10 Oct. 1994, 70.

11. Richard Yates, *Young Hearts Crying* (New York: Delacorte, 1984).

8. Force, Figures of Speech, and a Little Longinus

1. As adviser to Queen Zenobia of Palmyra, Asia Minor, Longinus was implicated in a conspiracy against Imperial Rome. Emperor Aurelius ordered the execution. Recent scholarship questions the authorship of *On Great Writing*, placing the treatise closer to the first century A.D.; but Longinus remains the brand-name author in references to the work. Citations here are from the G.M.A. Grube translation (New York: Liberal Arts Press, 1957).

2. Clyde Haberman, "Rabin Urges the Palestinians to Put Aside Anger and Talk," *The New York Times*, 1 March 1994, national edition.

3. Joan Didion, *A Book of Common Prayer* (New York: Simon & Schuster, 1977).

4. Molly Haskell, "Outing James Dean," *The New York Times Book Review*, 7 Aug. 1994.

5. Erich Maria Remarque, *Arch of Triumph* (New York: Appleton-Century, 1945). Remarque was a longtime friend of Dietrich.

6. Kazuo Ishiguro, *The Remains of the Day* (New York: Knopf, 1989).

9. Make My Day: The Power of Tough Talk

1. Jay Wilbur, business manager of Id Software, quoted by Peter Lewis, "Virtual Mayhem and Real Profits," *The New York Times*, 3 Sept. 1994.

2. Anna Quindlen, "Two Class Acts," *The New York Times*, 12 Nov. 1994.

3. For those who would immerse themselves in malediction high and low, *Maledicta: The International Journal of Verbal Aggression* (Maledicta Press, Santa Rosa, Calif., biennial) "specializes in uncensored studies and glossaries of offensive and negatively valued words and expressions, from all languages and cultures, past and present" (from masthead). Among the topics it deals with—in both scholarly and popular presentations—are verbal abuse, curses, scatology, slurs, stereotypes, graffiti, gestures, and murder and suicide. Not for the prudish, *Maledicta* is a rich and often entertaining record of antisocial expression.

4. Of many options, I chose the *Saint Joseph Edition of the Holy Bible* (New York: Catholic Book Publishing Co., 1963) for its spirited translation of this chapter by the New Contrafraternity of Christian Doctrine.

5. Jack Lessenberry, "The Lawyer Who Keeps the Suicide Doctor Free," *The New York Times*, 9 July 1993.

6. *Maledicta* (see Note 3) 10 (1988–89):246; 5 (summer/winter 1981):116.

7. Anthony Burgess, *A Mouthful of Air* (New York: William Morrow, 1992).

8. Overseas, the f-word gained in literary status when Scottish writer James Kelman won Britain's coveted Booker Prize for his novel *How Late It Was, How Late* (1994; U.S. edition, Norton, 1995). The 374-page book, a monologue, contains an estimated four thousand f-words.

9. In late 1995 Random House gathered, into a 224-page book called *The F-Word,* all the appearances of f*ck and its derivatives in the full database of the *Random House Historical Dictionary of American Slang.* The spin-off book was promoted as "the perfect gift for the word user . . . in every family."

10. David Mamet, *Glengarry Glen Ross* (New York: Grove Press, 1984), 19.

11. Martin Scorsese and Nicholas Pileggi, *GoodFellas* (screenplay), based on the book *Wiseguy* by Nicholas Pileggi. David Thompson, ed. (Boston: Faber and Faber, 1990). ©Warner Bros.

12. Richard Price, *Clockers* (New York: Houghton Mifflin, 1992).

13. "A Conversation About Slang with J. E. Lighter and Jesse Sheidlower," interview prepared by Nolan/Lehr Group, New York, issued as press release, ca. August 1994.

10. Model Expression: In Search of Paradigms

1. As quoted by Hilton Als in "The Only One," *The New Yorker,* 7 Nov. 1994, 106.

2. Deborah Tannen, *You Just Don't Understand: Women and Men in Conversation* (New York: William Morrow, 1990). In this and other works, Tannen calls the men's conversational model "report-talk" or "public speaking," talking as a way to get attention. The women's model, termed "rapport-talk" or "private speaking," emphasizes the display of similarities and matching of experiences; it is most comfortably performed among close connections.

3. Arthur Edward Phillips, *Natural Drills in Expression, with Selections* (Chicago: The Newton Co., 1913).

4. Philip Roth, *Operation Shylock* (New York: Simon & Schuster, 1993), 166.

5. Manny Trillo quoted in the *Chicago Tribune,* ca. June 1977.

6. Based on a 1988 study of Edward Taylor cited in *Dissertation Abstracts.*

7. *The New York Times,* 16 Aug. 1993.

8. *Inside* (Chicago), 12 May 1993.

9. Eliyahu M. Goldratt and Jeff Cox, "The Goal: A Process of Ongoing Improvement," *Journal of Business Strategy,* December 1993.

10. Derek Elley, "TV Reviews," *Variety,* 31 Oct.–6 Nov., 1994.

11. Jack Hart, "Trendspeak," *Editor & Publisher,* 13 Feb. 1993.

11. Other People's Words

1. Charles Curran, "Down with Slogans," *American Libraries*, December 1993.

12. Infusions for Tired Vocabularies

1. Reassembled phrases from "Mazzaroli's Cannon," by Peter Meinke, *Poetry*, February 1995.

2. Inspired by H. L. Mencken in 1925, *American Speech* has been sponsored since 1971 by the American Dialect Society, which researches language variations.

3. Among them, *The Barnhart Dictionary of New English Since 1963* (New York: Barnhart/Harper & Row, 1973); *12,000 Words: A Supplement to Webster's Third New International Dictionary* (Springfield, Mass.: Merriam-Webster, 1986); *Portmanteau Dictionary: Blend Words in the English Language* . . . , by Dick Thurner (Jefferson, N.C.: McFarland, 1993); *A Guide to the Oxford English Dictionary*, by Donna Lee Berg (Oxford: Oxford University Press, 1993); and "Changing American English in Times of Change," by Anne H. Soukhanov, *The Editorial Eye*, November 1993.

4. *The Random House Dictionary of the English Language*, 2d ed., unabridged, 1987, pp. 1026–27. I have shortened and otherwise adapted the dictionary's definitions for my commentaries.

5. Statement by Frank J. Biondi, Jr., president of Viacom, on dismissing the longtime chairman of Simon & Schuster. Sarah Lyall, "Viacom Acts to Calm Fears Over Dismissal of Snyder," *The New York Times*, 16 June 1994, national edition.

6. For years Roget had been gathering words arranged by concept and keeping a notebook to aid his own expression. At age sixty-seven he decided to bolster the world's way with words and began compiling a practical tool offering apt word choices for given contexts. His altruism and four years of labor "very much greater than I had anticipated" quickly paid off: The thesaurus went through twenty-eight editions in his lifetime. His son, artist John Roget, and then his grandson, electrical engineer Samuel Romilly Roget, kept the thesaurus up to date as editors. In 1952 the family sold its rights to the publisher Longmans, Green & Co.

7. Anthony Lane, *The New Yorker*, 30 Jan. 1995.

13. Specialized Words: Stimulation for Every Occasion

1. Andrew Sharp, *Winetaster's Secrets* (Toronto: Warwick, 1995).

2. Kathleen Odean, *High Steppers, Fallen Angels, and Lollipops* (New York: Henry Holt, 1989).

3. Connie Eble, *College Slang 101: A Definitive Guide to Words, Phrases, and Meanings They Don't Teach in English Class* (Georgetown, Conn.: Spectacle Lane Press, 1989). My definitions adapted from Eble. The book includes a brief sampling of Black English, which, like specialized gay vocabulary, animates undergraduate expression. See in Resources: Clarence Major, *Juba to Jive;* Geneva Smitherman, *Black Talk;* and Bruce Rodgers, *The Queens' Vernacular.*

4. ". . . *una noche toda llena de murmullos, de perfumes y de músicas de alas";* from "Nocturno," by José Asunción Silva (1865–96), the Colombian poet who took his life at thirty-one but left behind some of the richest love imagery in Western literature.

5. This line and the next one (Shaw) are from letters represented in *Famous Love Letters: Messages of Intimacy and Passion,* ed. by Ronald Tamplin (Pleasantville, N.Y.: Reader's Digest, 1995).

6. Margaret Sandburg, ed., *The Poet and the Dream Girl: The Love Letters of Lilian Steichen and Carl Sandburg* (Urbana, Ill., and Chicago: University of Illinois Press, 1987), 66, 68.

7. Mark Leyner, Introduction to *Tooth Imprints on a Corn Dog* (New York: Harmony Books, 1995).

8. Molly Katz, *Jewish as a Second Language* (New York: Workman, 1991).

9. Bill Bryson, *Neither Here nor There* (New York: Morrow, 1991).

14. Speaking Louder than Words: Oral Presentation

1. Among the purveyors of the ratio: Albert Mehrabian, *Silent Messages* (Belmont, Calif.: Wadsworth, 1971), 43.

2. Referred to but not cited in Bettye Pierce Zoller et al., *Power Talk: Standard American English, Your Ladder to Success* (Dallas: ZWL Publishing, 1994), 46.

3. Nick Jordan, "The Face of Feeling," *Psychology Today,* January 1986. Cited in Jess Scott Cook, *The Elements of Speechwriting and Public Speaking* (New York: Macmillan, 1990), 160. Even in huge convention ballrooms, audiences can see facial close-ups, thanks to a new fixture: live video of the speaker, projected to heroic proportions on a stage screen. The camera pulls back to show gestures, zooms in to magnify facial nuances.

4. Ben Brantley, "A Monologuist's Idiosyncratic Trip Through Disease and Healing." Review of *Gray's Anatomy* at Lincoln Center. *The New York Times,* 29 Nov. 1993.

5. Bender, Peter Urs. *Secrets of Power Presentations* (Buffalo: Firefly Books, 1995).

Afterword: Putting Thoughts into Digits

1. "Netiquette" is claimed as a trademark by Albion Books, San Francisco. See Resources.

2. Chip Bayer, managing editor, describing *Hotwired.* Quoted in "The Digerati!" by Paul Keegan, *The New York Times Magazine,* 21 May 1995.

3. Douglas Rushkoff, *Media Virus!* (New York: Ballantine, 1994).

4. Nicholas Negroponte, *Being Digital* (New York: Knopf, 1995).

5. Clifford Stoll, *The Cuckoo's Egg* (New York: Doubleday, 1989), and *Silicon Snake Oil: Second Thoughts on the Information Highway* (New York: Doubleday, 1995).

6. James Gleick, "Net Losses: Cyberhype Gives Way to Cybergripe in Unexpected Realms," *The New Yorker,* 22 May 1995.

7. David Angell and Brent Heslop, *The Elements of E-mail Style: Communicate Effectively via Electronic Mail* (Reading, Mass.: Addison-Wesley, 1994).

Resources

*T*o light your way to expressiveness, here are some one hundred language resources selected from the galactic mass. They range from enduring classics to the evanescent offerings of the Internet. In general, seek the latest editions or versions, but be aware that electronic versions may differ from print counterparts in coverage and strengths. Reference librarians can help track out-of-print and other elusive items. Not all subtitles are given here.
—*A.P.*

English and Language in General

The American Language. 4th ed. (1936) and the two supplements (1945, 1948), abridged. H. L. Mencken, with annotation and new material by Raven I. McDavid, Jr., assisted by David W. Maurer. New York: Knopf, 1967. Mencken's ground-breaking, masterly study of American English and the intertwining of language and culture.

The Cambridge Encyclopedia of Language. David Crystal. New York: Cambridge, 1987. A sprawling, illustrated treasury covering sixty-five themes of language study. Animated by the amiable style of this erudite British linguist.

The Cambridge Encyclopedia of the English Language. David Crystal. New York: Cambridge, 1995. Another Crystal treasure (see previous item), this one in four-color. An amazement to read and behold, with examples drawn equally from British and American English. Vast, brilliant, accessible.

The Language Instinct. Steven Pinker. New York: William Morrow, 1994. A stimulating discourse by a cognitive neuroscientist with a bright style. Evolution has hard-wired the language instinct into our brains, says Pinker, as he explores the ramifications.

The Miracle of Language. Richard Lederer. New York: Pocket Books, 1991. Essays on the efficiency, etymology, and idiosyncrasies of English by the popular verbivore.

The Mother Tongue: English and How It Got That Way. Bill Bryson. New York: Avon Books, 1990. The wisecracking travel writer voyages through beloved terrain.

A Mouthful of Air: Languages, Languages . . . Especially English. Anthony Burgess. New York: William Morrow, 1992. A scholar's eye and novelist's ear for the history and dynamics of language. Chapters include "Low-Life Language."

Paradigms Lost: Reflections on Literacy and Its Decline. John Simon. New York: Clarkson Potter, 1980. The acerbic critic is among the most engaging of the language conservatives.

Style, Usage, and Grammar

American Usage and Style: The Consensus. Roy H. Copperud. New York: Von Nostrand Reinhold, 1979. A reliable A-to-Z synthesis of what several major dictionaries and guides have to say on usage problems.

The Chicago Manual of Style. 14th ed. Chicago: University of Chicago, 1993. Practically a U.S. national standard for mechanical style in scholarly to general-audience publishing. Punctuation, numbers, bibliographies, footnotes, etc.

The Columbia Guide to Standard American English. Kenneth G. Wilson. New York: Columbia, 1993. With some 6,500 readable entries, a balanced (mainly nonprescriptive) guide to usage in current American written and spoken language.

The Deluxe Transitive Vampire: A Handbook of Grammar for the Innocent, the Eager, and the Doomed. Karen Elizabeth Gordon. New York: Pantheon, 1993. Gordon invents campy gothic examples to teach the workings of sentence structure.

The Elements of E-mail Style. David Angell and Brent Heslop. Reading, Mass.: Addison-Wesley, 1994. A blend of conventional composition principles and special advice for electronic communications, including network etiquette, politics, jargon. *Netiquette* (Virginia Shea. San Francisco: Albion, 1994) is another popular guide to on-line behavior, focusing more on protocol and ethics than on language mechanics.

Grammar for Grownups. Val Dumond. New York: HarperCollins, 1993. Inviting, intelligent approach that overcomes childhood misconceptions about grammar.

Guidelines for Bias-Free Writing. Marilyn Schwartz and the Task Force on Bias-Free Language of the Association of American Presses. Bloomington: Indiana University Press, 1995. Careful thinking as of 1995 on sensitive areas of language, especially in an academic context. Problem-by-problem advice supplements guides by Val Dumond (Prentice-Hall) and Casey Miller and Kate Swift (HarperCollins).

Harper Dictionary of Contemporary Usage. Edited by William and Mary Morris. 2d ed. New York: HarperCollins, 1992. Other guides cover more terms, but here a panel of well-known and opinionated word users sound off and "vote" on usage controversies.

Modern American Usage: A Guide. Wilson Follett. Edited and completed by Jacques Barzun and others. New York: Hill & Wang, 1966; Avenel, 1980. Word guidance and mini-essays in alphabetical order; a classic of firm rulings in an American context.

The New York Public Library Writer's Guide to Style and Usage. Edited by Andrea J. Sutcliffe. New York: HarperCollins, 1994. Prepared by EEI, a consulting group with years of real-life experience in helping writers and editors. Generous in scope, modern and sensitive in points of view. A writer's *Chicago Manual.*

The Oxford Dictionary of English Grammar. Edited by Sylvia Chalker and Edmund Weiner. New York: Oxford, 1994. An ambitious A-to-Z collection of some thousand terms from grammar and related studies, with definitions, cross-references, illustrative quotes, notes on American and other special usages.

Write Right! 3d ed. Jan Venolia. Berkeley, Calif.: Ten Speed Press, 1988. A consistently popular handbook of grammar, punctuation, and spelling.

Dictionaries

The American Heritage Dictionary of the English Language. 3d ed. Boston: Houghton Mifflin, 1992. (Parent of *The American Heritage College Dictionary,* 3d ed., 1993.) Expert lexicography in an appealing format, with some five hundred usage notes from a panel of notables. Definitions are in order of frequency of use.

The Barnhart Concise Dictionary of Etymology. Edited by Robert K. Barnhart. New York: HarperCollins, 1995. Authoritative, well written; explains the origins and development of some 25,000 "core" English words.

Merriam-Webster's Collegiate Dictionary. 10th ed. Springfield, Mass.: Merriam-Webster, 1993. Spawn of *Webster's Third New International Dictionary of the English Language, Unabridged* (1961, 1986), it draws on M-W's vast file of cited examples (quotes). Definitions in order of historical use. Style handbook included.

The Oxford English Dictionary. 2d ed. 20 vols. Oxford: Oxford, 1989. Supplemented about every two years by *Oxford English Dictionary Additions Series.* The ultimate English word source. Defines some half million words used from Chaucer's time to the present. "Diachronic" (details historical use of words) and descriptive (nonjudgmental); contains some 2.5 million illustrative quotations.

Random House Unabridged Dictionary. 2d ed. New York: Random House, 1993. Updated revision of *The Random House Dictionary of the English Language* (2d ed., 1987). An attractive major work influenced by lexicographer Stuart Berg Flexner. Liberal in admitting new words. Definitions in order of most common meanings.

Thesauruses

Roget's Thesaurus of Words and Phrases. Rev. ed. by Peter M. Roget. New York: Putnam, 1989. Stemming from Roget's 1852 original. A profusion of related words and phrases (and their opposites) grouped by concept in a progressive order, with an index to every term. (See discussion, Chapter 12.)

Roget's International Thesaurus. 5th ed. Edited by Robert L. Chapman. New York: HarperCollins, 1992. Another worthy heir to the original, with old categories expertly revamped and such new categories as fitness and computer science.

The Oxford Thesaurus: American Edition. Laurence Urdang. New York: Oxford, 1992. Combines the (more stimulating) conceptual organization with a handy A-to-Z arrangement of headwords. 250,000-word synonym index.

Guides to Prose Expression

The Describer's Dictionary. David Grambs. New York: Norton, 1993. What's the word for having a long nose? *Leptorrhine.* Like other reverse dictionaries, this one leads from loose to precise (describing) terms. But in addition, every opposite page offers model descriptive passages from literature. Focuses on observable phenomena.

Edit Yourself. Bruce Ross Larson. New York: W. W. Norton, 1982. Probably the best gathering of actual revisions favored by most editors, arranged for easy look-up.

The Elements of Style with Index. 3d ed. William Strunk, Jr., and E. B. White. New York: Macmillan, 1979. The dictatorial "little book" of usage and style advice (ca. 1959) is becoming dated, even by conservative standards. But for quick jabs at muddled expression, it still rules in its weight class.

First Paragraphs. Donald Newlove. New York: Henry Holt, 1992. A writer's fevered, instructive analysis of opening paragraphs by forceful writers. Why they work. Companion volumes: *Painted Paragraphs* (1993), exploring description, and *Invented Voices* (1994), on dialogue.

Honk If You're a Writer. Arthur Plotnik. New York: Simon & Schuster, 1992. Writing is edited crying, says the author. A wry journey through the literary pursuit.

It Was a Dark and Stormy Night: The Final Conflict. Compiled by Scott Rice. New York: Penguin, 1992. Winning entries from the ongoing Bulwer-Lytton bad-fiction contest make this a perverse how-not-to series, full of laughably rotten examples.

The New Oxford Guide to Writing. Thomas S. Kane. New York: Oxford, 1988. A rhetoric with heart by a longtime writing teacher. Covers creative and mechanical style.

On Great Writing (On the Sublime). Longinus. Trans. by G. M. A. Grube. New York: Liberal Arts Press, 1957. The classical critic's "five causes of great writing" endure, as does the charm of this surviving fragment. (See discussion, Chapter 8.)

On Writing Well. 5th ed. William Zinsser. New York: HarperCollins, 1994. A widely used standard on writing various forms of nonfiction, with modern examples. Zinsser advocates—and writes—prose that works without laboring.

Toward Clarity and Grace. Joseph M. Williams. Chicago: University of Chicago, 1990 (rev.). Intensive training for the intermediate-to-advanced writer. Acclaimed for its painstaking method of guiding clumsy prose toward good writing.

Writing with Precision. 6th ed. Jefferson Bates. Washington, D.C.: Acropolis, 1993. Brief, modular lessons on purposeful writing. Originally a textbook for managers.

Writer's Digest Books. Publishers of practical and inspirational writers' guides, such as *Discovering the Writer Within: 40 Days to More Imaginative Writing.* Catalog available from F&W Publications, 1507 Dana Ave., Cincinnati, OH 45207.

Prose Stylists

Note: We learn from models. In my chapters I have cited a number of exemplary prose stylists; the literary media unveil dozens more each season. Here I offer just a few personal choices that strayed from my text and endnotes.

A Book of Condolences: From the Private Letters of Illustrious People. Edited by

Rachel Harding and Mary Dyson. New York: Continuum, 1981. Models of the most difficult of all prose endeavors: words to console the bereaved.

The Art of the Personal Essay: An Anthology from the Classical Era to the Present. Edited by Phillip Lopate. New York: Doubleday/Anchor, 1994. A cornucopia of international excellence; fifty essays introduced by Lopate's essay on the form.

The Bible. Any standard Bible models the art of elevated narrative. The style of the King James Authorized Version of 1611—the Jacobean English of its forty-seven scholars—is, as Anthony Burgess says, the one "branded into the brain" for its Oriental flavor, literary grandeur, succinctness, and force *(A Mouthful of Air).*

The Color Purple. Alice Walker. New York: Harcourt Brace Jovanovich, 1982. "I make myself wood. I say to myself, Celie, you a tree." Walker has the ear, the gift.

Fever: Twelve Stories. John Edgar Wideman. New York: Henry Holt, 1989. A show of Wideman's range, from street funk to soaring levels of consciousness.

A House for Mr. Biswas. V. S. Naipaul. New York: Knopf, 1983. Exemplary for the music of its dialect. The versatile Naipaul calls this novel "the one closest to me."

House of Games: The Complete Screenplay. Based on a story by David Mamet and Jonathan Katz. New York: Grove Press, 1987. Visceral dialogue. "You came back like a dog to its vomit," says the protagonist to his avenging lover.

The House of the Spirits. Isabel Allende. Translated by Magda Bogin. New York: Knopf, 1985. Soul-stirring imagery, as generous as a banquet with "a scandalous number of whole steers . . . , birds stuffed with truffles, a torrent of exotic liquors. . . ."

Lost in the Cosmos: The Last Self-Help Book. Walker Percy. New York: Farrar, Straus, Giroux, 1983. Percy's sly wisdom in a parodic style, often as gnomic as his fiction in expressing the human condition. "Boredom is the self being stuffed with itself."

The Oxford Book of Letters. Edited by Frank and Anita Kermode. New York: Oxford, 1995. Spanning five centuries, some three hundred choice letters from the famous and obscure.

The Shipping News. E. Annie Proulx. New York: Scribner's, 1993. A modern novel set in Newfoundland. Fresh images pound and overflow the pages.

The Snow Leopard. Peter Matthiessen. New York: Viking Penguin, 1978. A masterpiece of hard-won observation—sensual and spiritual—in the high Himalayas.

The Stone Diaries. Carol Shields. New York: Viking Penguin, 1994. Novelist as omniscient observer of a life, birth to death, with mastery of telling word and image. "Now she's like some great department store of sadness with . . . silent reflecting windows, out of business, the padlock on the door."

A Thousand Acres. Jane Smiley. New York: Knopf, 1991. Style that perfectly complements its fictional subject (farm-family tragedy), never intruding.
The Volcano Lover. Susan Sontag. New York: Farrar, Straus, Giroux, 1992. A distinctive narrative approach to the historical novel, skillful in its shifts of voice.
Wonder Boys. Michael Chabon. New York: Villard, 1995. Stylistic zingers are everywhere in Chabon's novels. "Undressing her was an act of recklessness, a kind of vandalism, like releasing a zoo full of animals, or blowing up a dam."

Quotations

General *(See also discussion of sources in Chapter 11)*

The Columbia Dictionary of Quotations. Robert Andrews. New York: Columbia, 1993. Claiming eleven thousand "new" quotations out of its eighteen thousand total, *Columbia* is a good source for fresh twentieth-century quotes. Alphabetical by narrow subject, with author index.
Familiar Quotations. 16th ed. Compiled by John Bartlett and edited by Justin Kaplan. New York: Little, Brown, 1992. Published since 1855, noted for its thoughtful selection and attention to historical sources. Author and keyword indexes.
The Home Book of Quotations, Classical and Modern. 10th ed. Burton Stevenson. New York: Dodd, Mead, 1967. With fifty thousand quotes arranged by subject and indexed by keyword, this standard yields something—if not the latest quip—for every occasion.
The International Thesaurus of Quotations. Revised and updated. Eugene Ehrlich and Marshall De Bruhl. New York: HarperCollins, 1995. Some sixteen thousand pithy quotations under one thousand topical headings, each with cross-references to related and opposing headings. A fine source for getting to the right words. Keyword, author indexes.

Specialized

A Dictionary of Literary Quotations. Merc Stephens. New York: Routledge, 1990. "Books succeed,/And lives fail."—Elizabeth Barrett Browning. Collected for decades by the compiler, 3,250 choice quotes about literature, writing, and related areas.
Leo Rosten's Treasury of Jewish Quotations. New York: McGraw-Hill, 1972. Rosten's commentary on Jewish/Yiddish expression, with 4,352 brief examples he collected.
My Soul Looks Back, 'Less I Forget: A Collection of Quotations by People of Color. Edited by Dorothy Winbush Riley. New York: HarperCollins, 1993. The seven

thousand quotations mined by the compiler help balance the whiteness of most standard collections.

Special Lexicons and Word Treasuries

The American Thesaurus of Slang. 2d ed. Lester B. Berrey and Melvin Van den Bark. New York: Crowell, 1953. An update of the huge 1942 grouping of terms by concept (Part 1) and (Part 2) special fields, such as Eating Establishments.

Black Talk: Words and Phrases from the Hood to the Amen Corner. Geneva Smitherman. New York: Houghton Mifflin, 1994. Terms in current use, with many vivid examples and an edifying introduction by the compiler.

The Book of Jargon. Don Ethan Miller. New York: Macmillan, 1982. Decodes the "in" language of twenty-five specialized areas, Auto Mechanics to New Age Therapies.

Brewer's Dictionary of Phrase and Fable. 15th ed. Edited by Ivor H. Evans. New York: HarperCollins, 1995. A standard. Meanings and origins of some twenty thousand intriguing terms and phrases from Aaron's Beard to Zen, with charming discourse and quotes.

Concise Dictionary of Foreign Expressions. Compiled by B. A. Phythian. Totowa, N.J.: Barnes & Noble, 1982. Many are the foreign-expression guides available separately or as dictionary appendixes. This oldie is solid, if not the *dernier cri.*

Concise Science Dictionary. New York: Oxford, 1984. *Pelagic. Isostasy.* A handy starting place for humanists eager to loot the riches of science terminology.

Dickson's Word Treasury: A Connoisseur's Collection of Old & New, Weird & Wonderful, Useful & Outlandish Words. Paul Dickson. New York: Wiley, 1992. Dickson's collections delight even *dunderwhelps* (see under "Loutish Words").

The Facts on File Visual Dictionary. Jean-Claude Corbeil. New York: Facts on File, 1986. Thousands of natural and manufactured objects and parts are pictured and named in visual dictionaries, useful for learning nomenclature in native or foreign languages. What do you call the thing that hits the "lip" of a bell? (The "clapper.")

Fifty Years Among the New Words: A Dictionary of Neologisms, 1941–1991. Edited by John Algeo. New York: Cambridge 1991. (See discussion, Chapter 12.) A masterly introduction to new-word formation, plus commentary (extracted from *American Speech)* on about four thousand terms, *blitz* (1940) to *boy toy* (1990).

Happy as a Clam and 9,999 Other Similes. Larry Wright. New York: Macmillan, 1994. *Like* and *as* comparison phrases arranged under almost two thousand A-to-Z categories.

Juba to Jive: A Dictionary of African-American Slang. Edited by Clarence Major.

New York: Viking Penguin, 1994. Modern and historical slang associated with African Americans, gathered by poet and novelist Major and supplementing other sources.

Listening to America. Stuart Berg Flexner. New York: Simon & Schuster, 1982. Sequel to the lexicographer's *I Hear America Talking* (1976), both works chronicling the voice of the *free-for-all* (1902) American culture. A word person's take on U.S. history.

The New Hacker's Dictionary. 2d ed. Edited by Eric S. Raymond. Cambridge, Mass.: MIT Press, 1993. (See discussion, Chapter 13.) The authority. Some three thousand terms from the computer and cyberspace cultures; extensive, zany definitions.

Poplollies and Bellibones: A Celebration of Lost Words. Susan Kelz Sperling. New York: Clarkson N. Potter, 1977. Obsolete words deserving new life. (Title words: "little darlings" and "lovely maidens.") The author "expects to snirtle and keak over the woodness of words, either in hudder-mudder or with fellowfeeling boonfellows. . . ."

The Queens' Vernacular: A Gay Lexicon. Bruce Rodgers. San Francisco: Straight Arrow Books, 1972. A "passionately gathered" collection of comic, biting, highly metaphoric terminology. Rodgers provides expressive usage examples.

Random House Dictionary for Writers and Readers. David Grambs. New York: Random House, 1990. A literate, endearing collection of some two thousand terms about language and literature, with many usage examples. Includes twenty-four special glossaries, such as Blurb Adjectives—Rousing! Towering! Sweeping!

Random House Historical Dictionary of American Slang. Vol. 1, A–G. Edited by J. E. Lighter. New York: Random House, 1994. (Vols. 2, H–R, and 3, S–Z, sched. 1996–97.) The three volumes constitute the largest and finest such collection, with more than 50,000 terms and 200,000 examples of historical use—providing an enormous stock of salty quotes. Scholarly and fascinating. (See discussion, Chapter 9.)

Random House Word Menu. Stephen Glazier. New York: Random House, 1992. Lists of contemporary words, with brief definitions, under subject categories. A vast collection, excellent for tracking forgotten or undiscovered names of things.

Reader's Digest Success with Words: A Guide to the American Language. Pleasantville, N.Y.: Reader's Digest, 1983. Misleadingly titled, this A-to-Z miscellany of usage, dialect, and language principles and lore has more to do with learning and delight than "success." Typical entry: five enlightening pages on "Hawaiian English."

Similes Dictionary. Detroit: Gale Research, 1988. Library publisher Gale specializes in large compilations, such as this one of more than 16,000 similes. Gale's Visible Ink Press issues bookstore versions, e.g., . . . *As One Mad with*

Wine and Other Similes (1991) and *Metaphors Dictionary* (1995) with 6,500 metaphoric comparisons.

Word Watch: The Stories Behind the Words of Our Lives. Anne H. Soukhanov. New York: Henry Holt, 1995. The language editor and columnist explores 365 new words and phrases reflecting societal patterns—*red-diaper baby* (born of U.S. leftists, 1913–60), *plop art* (corporate-sponsored art plopped in public places), and *blendo* (mix of interior decorating styles) among them. Zesty afterword on language evolution.

Oral and Nonverbal Expression

The Elements of Speechwriting and Public Speaking. Jeff Scott Cook. New York: Macmillan, 1990. Agile speechwriter Cook presents the fundamentals of writing and giving talks. An intelligent primer with many tips and good examples.

The Nonverbal Communications Reader. Joseph A. DeVito and Michael L. Hecht. Prospect Heights, Ill.: Waveland Press, 1989. A comprehensive, readable textbook.

Power Talk: Standard American English—Your Ladder to Success. Bettye Pierce Zoller, John Arthur Watkins, and Hugh Lampman. Dallas: ZWL Publishing, 1994. (Book and three audiocassettes.) English-first politics aside, these self-study materials deliver the goods for speech improvement, with many articulation exercises.

Signals: How to Use Body Language for Power, Success, and Love. Allan Pease. New York: Bantam, 1984. A popular synthesis on the meanings of physical gestures and positions, well illustrated. Worth reading before the next job interview.

Smart Speaking: Sixty-Second Strategies. Laurie Schloff and Marcia Yudkin. New York: Henry Holt, 1991. A compassionate problem-by-problem approach to confidence and control. E.g., "I'm not Funny, Eloquent, or Interesting—Is There Any Hope for Me?"

Speak with Distinction. Edith Skinner. Revised by Timothy Monich and Lilene Mansell. Edited by Lilene Mansell. New York: Applause, 1990. "The classic Skinner method to speech on the stage." Advice plus thousands of speech-sound drills.

Talking from 9 to 5: Women and Men in the Workplace: How Women's and Men's Conversational Styles Affect Who Gets Heard, Who Gets Credit, and What Gets Done at Work. Deborah Tannen. (See also Note 2, Chapter 10.) New York: William Morrow, 1994. A Tannen close-up of talk dynamics and how they determine status.

What to Say When You're Dying on the Platform. Lilly Walters. New York: McGraw-Hill, 1995. Crowd-pleasing cover-up lines for 130 nightmarish speaker's situations.

Journals

American Speech: A Quarterly of Linguistic Usage. Tuscaloosa: University of Alabama Press. Specialized articles plus John and Adele Algeo's celebrated "Among the New Words" column. (See *Fifty Years Among the New Words,* above.)

Editorial Eye. Monthly newsletter. Alexandria, Va.: EEI. Editorial consultants and guest contributors address issues of form and content in publishing. Lively, practical.

English Today. Quarterly journal. New York: Cambridge. News about English from academic and journalistic perspectives. New-word sightings are among its tidbits.

Maledicta. Biennial journal. Santa Rosa, Calif.: Maledicta Press. (See Note 3, Chapter 9.) Observations of aggressive and erotic language; multicultural.

Verbatim. Quarterly, newsletter format. Old Lyme, Conn.: Verbatim. Drawn by the light of editor Laurence Urdang, word-wise contributors make *Verbatim* a center of expert and often playful language commentary, debate, and collection.

Electronic Resources

Note: As of late 1995, many of the standard, data-rich language guides cited above were in or headed for CD-ROM and pay on-line versions. We need not list these electronic titles individually. Such versions usually add interactive features and powerful search options. Some add graphics and audio, such as pronunciation. Free Internet versions are often samplers of or teasers for the fee-based products. Often, print versions remain a sensible option for scope, readability, convenience, and cost.

CD-ROMs

Microsoft Bookshelf '95. Redmond, Wash.: Microsoft, 1995. An eight-book reference package that includes versions of these language tools: *American Heritage Dictionary,* with audio pronunciation, *The Original Roget's Thesaurus,* and *The Columbia Dictionary of Quotations.* Easy to use and affordable for individuals.

Toolworks Reference Library. Novato, Calif.: The Software Toolworks. Another affordable package, including the dictionary, thesaurus, and quotable definitions from the *Webster's New World* group and *The Guide to Concise Writing.*

Quotations and poetry. Chapter 11 names several CD-ROM collections of quotations and poems. Most can retrieve buckets of quotes by subject, keyword, phrase, or author. Here we add *Gale's Quotations: Who Said What?*

Detroit: Gale Research, 1995 (117,000 quotations, updating earlier version); *The Columbia Granger's World of Poetry 1995, on CD-ROM.* New York: Columbia, 1995 (135,000 poems by more than 20,000 poets); and *Database of African-American Poetry, 1760–1900, on CD-ROM.* Alexandria, Va.: Chadwyck-Healey, 1994. (A unique collection of 2,500 poems.)

World's Greatest Speeches. Irvine, Calif.: Softbit. Text of four hundred speeches, Moses to Clinton, with two hours of audio, thirty minutes of video, and search software.

Disk Software

WritePro. Scarborough, N.Y.: The WritePro Corp. A popular tutorial, with prompting, mentoring, and tricks of the trade for fiction writers especially.

Grammar and style checkers. Adequate versions are often bundled with major word-processing packages. Version 5 of *Grammatik* (Orem, Utah: Word-Perfect) has sold over 1.5 million and is one of the best, says Hy Bender in *Essential Software for Writers* (Cincinnati: Writer's Digest Books, 1994).

The Internet

The World-Wide Web Virtual Library: Writers' Resources on the Web. A homebase index that points or automatically links users to all known writing-related sites on the Web and other Internet environments, including Gopher and Usenet. New links are constantly added. Use your Web browser to get to the "WWW Virtual Library" and choose "Writer's Resources on the Web" to unveil the index. Or, for direct linkage, address the following URL (Uniform Resource Locator):

http://www.interlog.com/˜ ohi/www/writesource.html

You will then see a menu of dozens of choices, such as "Steve's Rhetoric and Writing Page" and "Writer's Source." Clicking on these choices leads to more layers and finally to actual information or discussion on writing and language. "The Word" turned out to be a rich source, "English Server" an interesting one. Several choices lead to on-line composition workshops.

Most Usenet chat groups on writing and usage are unmoderated and anarchic; anyone can enter the electronic parlor and say anything. Few of the "postings" will make you more expressive—except in malediction—but sometimes questions to the group get a useful answer. Among groups worth checking out are **alt.usage.english** and **bit.listserv.words-l.** With the subject-browsing tools of your system you will sight flocks of chat groups on literary topics as well as more serious language-discussion groups to which one subscribes (listserves), such as **ads-l** of the American Dialect Society.

The Information Highway can be wearying. For quick comic relief, try this site: **jive@ifi.unizh.ch.** Mail a brief message there, and almost instantly your words come back translated into a funky old jive. I wrote: "You are unfailingly expressive. May you endure for the delectation of my readers." The response: "You's are unfailin'ly espressive. What it is, Mama! May ya' endure fo' mah eyeballers."

And may mah eyeballers endure.

Index